MONKEY MOMENTS

MONKEY MOMENTS

Encounters in Rainforest Escapades

GHAZALLY ISMAIL

To order additional copies of this book, contact:
Xlibris
NZ TFN: 0800 008 756 (Toll Free inside the NZ)
NZ Local: 9-801 1905 (+64 9801 1905 from outside New Zealand)
www.Xlibris.co.nz
Orders@Xlibris.co.nz
834432

CONTENTS

PREFACE

For more than four decades as an academician, I have been making something of a specialty writing about science and the environment. I've never thought of writing about myself. I still harbour mixed feelings about writing an autobiography despite constant encouragement from friends and former students. The whole genre on memoirs and life stories seems like an exercise of self-aggrandisement. But in some respects, writing about my own experience and reflecting on them would be of great convenience. It saves me from doing research on other people's works. Furthermore, I could never misquote myself or be accused of plagiarism. I'm still confused about quoting and plagiarising. It's plagiarism if I use one source but considered research if I use more than one source in my writing. Admittedly, laziness also tends to set in at my age. A more direct communication with my readers would get my message across faster and easier. Being a narrator of things others had said puts me on the periphery rather than the star of the show. Perhaps my readers need to hear the stories directly from the horse's mouth.

But a book about monkeys and apes? Really? Me, a microbiologist? I could just hear what would be playing on the minds of people who know my background and forte upon seeing this book. They all know me as a long-serving academic; my field of specialisation is microbiology and immunology. What gives? You don't actually think upon my retirement I would still be writing about bacteria and antibody, do you? What I know about those stuff would be outdated by now anyway. You do know I am also passionate about nature and environment. So writing about my personal experiences with nature wouldn't be as far-fetched. Musty and out of date they won't be. They might even be fashionable. My encounters and wisdom gained from being close to nature would live forever in my heart. I thought it would be fun to share them with readers who might have gone through the same experience.

Nature took up residence in my heart since I moved to Sabah in 1981. The flora and fauna of Borneo consumed a big chunk of available space in my heart yet left enough room to pursue my formal field of training in microbiology and immunology. Soon enough, I found myself loving animals as much as I did for bacteria, fungi, and viruses. Ironical but true. I delighted in seeing animals in the wild. I loved to watch the affection and interaction between animals and their natural surroundings.

Throughout my four decades as an environmentalist, I hear piercing cries from the wilderness—blaring and distinctly clear, they are in deep distress. Animal species are desperately begging us to save them from extinction. Humans are destroying their rainforest habitats at an alarming rate. The animals fear for their future. It looks grim, and they want their forests back. Their hopes to continue surviving dashed. The most recent animal species pushed to extinction in Malaysia is the Sumatran rhinoceros, *Dicerorhinus sumatrensis*. Terrible and tragic. That should also serve as the ultimate wake-up call. We need to do more to save other iconic and critically endangered species. I feel it's time to give our voice to their plight. Help them from becoming extinct!

Starkly conspicuous in this book, I have attempted to present my fascination with monkeys and apes visually through my own sketches. From my heart, I have provided narrations of the species and issues affecting their continued survival in the wild. My drawings and texts double as my impassioned plea. For better understanding and taste of the majority, I have used non-technical tongue wherever appropriate.

My aim is to create a new and stronger awareness in everyone on the critical issues faced by primates in our rainforests. We are still grappling with their future. Amongst these issues include the ongoing reality of biodiversity loss, global warming, and newly emerging diseases we are experiencing today. As this book beseechingly aims to implore these issues, I invite you to share my enthusiasm and call for environment advocacy. Help put an end to biodiversity loss and degradation of natural habitats.

THE SPARKS STARTED HERE

I HAVE WALKED IN THE rainforest and sensed nature's peace from the flow of sunshine through the canopy falling on my neck. I have walked along a hundred beautiful lakes and rivers. I can still smell the sweet fragrance of blossoming shrubs along the water's edge. I can feel the mild breeze gently sweeping through my hair as I gaze nonchalantly at the opalescent dawns and saffron sunsets on many shores. The wilderness has given me blessed release from the constant anxiety and troubled thinking of our modern society. Nature has been providing me countless free return tickets to the primitive and the peaceful. Soon enough, I became addicted to the three things nature does for me: happiness, freedom, and peace of mind. The hustle-bustle of city life magically leaves me alone in absolute peace.

Whenever the pressure of complex city life thins my blood and benumbs my brain, I seek relief in the mountain trails and coral reefs under the caring arms of nature. My craving for wilderness is more than a hunger. It is also my expression of allegiance to Mother Earth—the master who had endured, taught, and sustained us all. She is the only paradise we shall ever know and ever need. Over the years, I have trained my eyes to see the wilderness as not a luxury but a necessity of my existence and selflessness.

Albert Einstein recognised our need to understand nature in his famous quote, 'Look deep into nature and then you will understand everything better.' When you fall in love with nature, you tend to love the whole integral part of nature—the physical and biological parts that make nature magnificent, beautiful, and functional. However, in the pursuit of my career as an academic, I found myself drawn more towards the biological aspects of nature. I became more fascinated with nature's species components, not much the geological and physical landscape. But I must admit I have been more appreciative of the heavenly landscapes and jagged rock features of my surrounding since living in New Zealand. The geological formations of 2 million years old can be jaw-dropping nevertheless. I couldn't help feeling a tad regretful and wished I had kept myself awake and more attentive in geology lectures during my undergraduate days at Otago University. Those morning lectures and headaches from previous night's parties just didn't go too well as far as I could recall. I would have enjoyed more walking on those bed of strange-looking rock formations at the beach today. I could have told interesting geological tales of what those pitted holes and thin lines in the rocks were supposed to be to my grandchildren. Instead, Grandpa seemed only interested in stuff that moved and capable of breeding. Instead of satiating their hunger for knowledge on nature around them, all I could offer my grandkids was fish-and-chips meals by the beach surrounded by hungry seagulls. In their minds, that only managed to trigger more questions than answers in areas of geology.

Being interested in the biological side of nature, my first inquisitiveness was directed towards knowing how many species exist. What other species of plants and animals are sharing and coexisting on this planet with us, *Homo sapiens*? A recent study from Indiana University, USA, suggests that there are nearly 1 trillion species on Earth. Only one-thousandth of 1 per cent have been identified. That only gives us some idea on the number of distinct species that make up life on this planet, not what they are. The truthful answer is we simply don't know. Current estimates for the number of species on Earth range between 5.3 million and 1 trillion. That's a massive degree of uncertainty. You just can't take such numbers seriously, can you? Would you even blink if you get a bank statement saying you have between $5.30 and $1 million in your account?

Part of the problem is the difficulty to count life. We cannot simply count the number of life forms because many live in inaccessible habitats. For instance, it is almost an impossibility still to venture into the deepest trenches of our seafloors, and oceans happen to make up 70 per cent of this planet we ironically call Earth. Many life forms are too small to see. Some are hard to find because they might be living inside other life forms. It is believed most, if not all, insect species harbour at least one or more species of parasitic wasps inside their body. These wasps lay eggs in or on their host species absolutely unnoticed, away from the scrutiny of scientists.

So, instead of counting, scientists are forced to estimate the total number of species by looking for patterns in biodiversity. For instance, in the early 1980s, the American entomologist Terry Erwin distinctively estimated the number of species on Earth by spraying pesticides into the canopy of tropical rainforest trees in Panama. He counted around 1,200 species of beetles fell to the ground, out of which 163 came from a single tree species. By assuming each tree species supported a similar number of beetles and that beetles made up about 40 per cent of all insects, Erwin arrived at a controversial estimate of 30 million species on Earth. Many scientists cast doubt on this saying 30 million was an overestimate. Later revisions of the number of species by other extrapolative methods put the figures under 10 million. More recent estimates in 2011 using a technique based on patterns in the number of species at each class of organisms, a much lower number of about 8.7 million species was obtained. But that estimate doesn't include life forms that are microscopically small. Most estimates of species on planet Earth chose not to include microorganisms such as bacteria and viruses because these living forms can only be identified to species level by sequencing their DNA. As a result, all estimations till then were much too low. The latest attempt made by the Indiana University researchers avoided this underestimation. They compiled and analysed a database of DNA sequences from 5 million microbial species from 35,000 sites around the world. They finally came to the conclusion that the number of species on planet Earth is a staggering 1 trillion. That's more species than the estimated number of stars in the Milky Way galaxy! Again, like previous estimates, this, too, relies on patterns in biodiversity. Not everyone agrees such estimate can be used to count species of microorganisms.

Another curious aspect of life forms on this planet is their distribution. Some species are found in abundance in certain locations but scarce or non-existent elsewhere. It's common knowledge that biodiversity increases as we move from the poles to the equator. Our tropical rainforest is one of the most diverse and richest in flora and fauna on Earth. Why? Many hypothesis have been proposed. There are both historical and ecological factors that could have generated and maintained high biodiversity in the tropics.

Tropical rainforests are probably the planet's oldest continuous ecosystems. They began to take form some 140 million years ago during the age of the dinosaurs. During this late Cretaceous period, much of the world's climate was tropical or subtropical. It was during this period that flowering plants literally took roots and began to spread across the globe. Ecosystem changes occurred throughout this long history when plant and animal species have come and gone. Along with the changes, new ecosystems and communities evolved. New relationships between biological and physical components of nature were forged. The plants and animals competed and adapted to survive and further their own species. In the process, variants and new species emerged.

Generally, the changes are relatively slow, although there have been times of upheaval where drastic changes occurred over a short period. These natural upheavals appear to foster an increase in biological diversity as evidenced by the effect of the ice ages, especially on the Malay Archipelago in Southeast Asia. Today, many of the 20,000 or so islands of the Malay Archipelago are covered with tropical forests. Some of these rainforests have existed in some form or another for the past 100 million years.

During the ice ages, ocean waters condensed or became frozen and locked up in the South and North Poles as ice. This resulted in the ocean floor to become shallow. The South China Sea was hugely exposed, increasing the size of the land mass. A network of land bridges was formed. Subsequently, these new land connections allowed animal species to roam all across mainland Asia to other parts of the region previously inundated by sea water. Along with them, plant seeds were carried and dispersed in these new areas. They inhabited these new areas and cross-bred. Over time and repeated pressures from subsequent ice ages, the original mainland species could be producing new variants of species. Genetic exchange from cross-breeding would ultimately result in the emergence of completely new plant and animal species.

When the ice ages came to an end, a warmer climate returned, and the ocean rose again to re-flood the shallow areas of the South China Sea. Many of the plants and animals that had crossed over from the mainland were trapped on the regenerated island habitats. In addition, some of the montane and more temperate plant species adapted to the gradually warming climate and became tropical species. The small pockets of tropical rainforest that survived the ice ages served as biological reservoirs to repopulate the new islands. Animal species that had been trapped and insulated in their new habitats would adapt to their new niches. Their physical features, dietary needs, and body physiology would over time become more suited to their new environment. They would continue to reproduce, and in due generational time, new distinct species are created.

For example, take a hypothetical elephant species that began as a single species on mainland Asia. During the ice ages, the lower ocean levels created land bridges to the mainland. This expanded the range of the elephants to some of the islands of the Malay Archipelago not reachable before the ocean levels became shallow. When the ice ages came to an end, the ocean levels were raised again. The elephants became stranded on the newly formed islands. On the smaller islands, those elephants with a smaller body size tended to survive and reproduce more successfully because their lower dietary requirements could be sustained by the smaller amount of food available on the island. The larger individuals tended to be less successful in meeting their food requirement and reproduce poorly as a result. Thus, evolution favoured the dwarfing of elephants on the islands over the course of several thousand years. When the next ice age came, the mainland elephants could have crossed over again. But this time. the dwarfed island elephants could have diverged enough genetically that they were no longer able to breed with the mainland elephants. It is easy to speculate that over the course of two or three ice ages, one species of elephant could have become two or three. Hence, the process of evolution could happen through geographic isolation and adaptation to result in new species. Indeed, this was how Borneo's pygmy elephants might have ended up a distinct population found in Sabah today. They were isolated from mainland Asian elephants when Borneo was cut off from the mainland around 18,000 years ago.

Borneo is estimated to be home to an amazing number of animal species, including 222 mammals. 420 birds, 100 amphibians, and 394 fishes. Equally remarkable is the number of endemic species or species not found anywhere else in the world. They include forty-four mammals, thirty-seven birds, and nineteen fishes. At the risk of repeating myself, let's consider specifically why Borneo has high number of endemic species. This high incidence of endemicity on Borneo island can be explained from what happened some 21,000 years ago. During that period, Borneo was connected to mainland Southeast Asia as part of a land mass known as Sundaland. Seawater level then was 150 metres shallower than presently. The islands of Philippines, Indonesia, Malaysia, and Singapore were all connected with mainland Asia. From 2.5 million years ago until some 10,000 years ago, the region experienced several cycles of climatic changes. The ice ages caused the oceans to freeze and trapped sea water as ice at the two polar ends of the Earth. As a result, the sea levels were lowered. When the Earth warms up again, the poles thawed, raising the ocean levels, but this time modifying the total area of the region. Many small and big islands were formed. Plant and animal species became isolated and over time adapted to the new environment to emerge as unique species found nowhere else. This was how endemic species were created. After the ice age ended, Borneo became such island where species from the mainland Asia were trapped and isolated from their parent breed. Adaptation in their food intake and physiologic features enabled them to survive and breed to ultimately emerge as a distinctly new endemic species.

Understanding and speculating how an endemic species could have emerged from existing groups of animals or plants seems straightforward. It makes sense and easily comprehended. A more challenging concept to grasp is how different groups of organisms come to exist. In the animal kingdom, for instance, how do frogs, fish, mammals, and birds come to be as distinctly different from one another? Today, we have come quite close in figuring this out or, at best, coming up with believable theories on the subject. Thanks to the discovery of useful clues through fossils left behind by earlier species inhabiting this same planet of ours.

Animal life on Earth began in the marine environment. Between 390 million and 360 million years ago, the first vertebrates began to crawl their way out from the sea onto land. They first adapted to live in shallower waters and eventually moved to land. These were descendants of the present-day terrestrial animals. Their fins evolved into limbs and gills into lungs to better adapt living in their new terrestrial environment. Out of the water, the pioneering fish had access to oxygenated air. Consequently, they could see better with their eyes no longer submerged in water. Their visual range increased substantially, enabling them to seek food far and wide. The animals with rudimentary limbs were naturally selected to continue surviving. With better chance of finding food, the species with limbs triumphed over others. It was the survival of the fittest. This adaptation was later followed with an increase in their eye size. Over the eons, the emergence of more advanced cognition and complex planning generally defined them as terrestrial animals.

For many of us, of all living things, animals are a constant source of fascination. Perhaps because we are animals ourselves. Amongst all animals, the mammals intrigue me most. I am sure this is because we possess a number of features in common compared to other groups in the animal kingdom like amphibians, birds, fish, invertebrates, and reptiles. These common mammalian features indicate that we have a shared evolutionary history.

One of the most remarkable things about nature is its resilience. The plant and animal species around us today have been evolving since there was life on Earth. Like the plants, animals evolved in the sea. At least 600 million years ago, the land portion on this planet Earth was not where life could have lasted long and survived. There was no ozone layer to protect life from the lethal levels of ultraviolet (UV) radiation bathing the Earth then. But when plants started to colonise the land, the atmospheric levels of oxygen were raised high enough for the protective ozone layer to be formed around the Earth's surface. That made possible for animals to venture onto the land safely without harm from the UV radiation. The oldest fossil evidence of multicellular animals were burrows that appeared to have been made by some wormlike organisms. Such trace fossils have been found in rocks from China, Canada, and India.

Since the 1800s, scientists and philosophers have been grappling with the question of how other multicellular organisms came to exist on planet Earth. Charles Darwin and Alfred Russel Wallace proposed evolution of species. Other multicellular species inhabiting Earth today came to existence through a phenomenon called natural selection. In their book *On the Origin of Species,* written in 1837, they presented the compelling theory of natural selection. It essentially stated that species produce more individuals that are able to survive better than the previous generations. Their offspring would have superior traits that are better suited for the environment, making them more successful to compete and survive. These superior attributes are termed as phenotypic variations. Further, the theory proposed that variation is heritable; meaning, it can be passed from one generation to another. The theory of natural selection and heritability of selected traits are today considered to be the foundation of evolutionary biology.

The extension of these two fundamental principles of evolution to how man came to being immediately became a far-reaching point of contention. It sparked the most controversial notion about the evolution of man that wasn't received well by the religionists of that era. According to Darwin's book *On the Origin of Species,* humans have evolved from apes. Most averse to Darwin's theory was the Catholic Church. The book of Genesis made no mention of humans evolving alongside orangutans, chimpanzees, bonobos, and gorillas. Neither was that mentioned in the Muslim's Holy Quran. Most Christians and Muslims outrightly reject this thought. This incompatibility about the origin of man between religion and evolution persisted till now.

Evolution and religious beliefs need not be in contradiction because they concern different matters. Religion and science both offer explanations for why life and the universe exist. They are two different windows for looking at the same world. Science is based on reasoning from observation such as how planets move, the composition of matter and the atmosphere, and the origin and adaptations of organisms. Science relies on testable empirical evidence and observation. Religion relies on subjective belief in the existence of the ultimate Creator. It concerns the meaning and purpose of the world and of human life. That requires a relationship of the believers with the Creator for the moral values to inspire and govern their lives.

Starting my career as an educator in the field of biology, I personally was caught in the midst of this pertinacious controversy. The late 1970s and early 1980s happened to be the beginning of the Islamic resurgence amongst Malays in Malaysia. Its influence was especially felt amongst those educated in the Western secular tradition. Whilst overseas, a number of Malay students formed a tacit alliance between the Malaysian Islamic Youth Movement (Angkatan Belia Islam Malaysia or ABIM) and the main Islamic opposition party, the Parti Islam Se Malaysia (PAS), which gave the resurgence a political momentum. The ruling National Front (Barisan Nasional) government needed to respond accordingly. The resurgence was countenanced by the Malaysian government through its own Islamisation program. Soon after, the academicians at local universities, including my own National University of Malaysia (UKM), were scrambling to channel the Islamic resurgence along a new path of disseminating secular knowledge. They were bending over backwards trying to inject Islamic perspectives in almost every subject taught at the university. As the dean of a faculty at UKM Sabah, I wasn't exempted from this ever-consuming trend of imparting knowledge through Islamic perspectives.

It didn't take long for my superiors from the main campus to pressure me into complying. They felt I was obligated to dance to the same tune. Hence, I was persistently asked to inculcate Islamic perspectives in all the science courses offered at my Faculty of Science and Natural Resources. For example, I was pressured by the chancellery in UKM main campus to ask my staff, mostly foreigners of other faiths, to stop teaching the theory of evolution to our students. To me, Darwin's theory of evolution and adaptation was the basis of our understanding species diversity and functions on planet Earth. How would we teach biology in the Faculty of Science and Natural Resources without telling our students about such a fundamental principle determining the existence of life around us? Those must have been amongst the days I would consider the most stressful times in my teaching career. I found the directive not only ludicrous but also an impossibility to execute amongst my teaching staff, who were mostly non-Muslims. Scientists are more likely to take some religious things a bit less literally. For instance, geologists probably wouldn't think that the Earth and everything else was actually made by God 6,000 years ago, since their science tells them that the Earth is 4.5 billion years old. I wasn't about to alter the facts to fit their views but was stoically adamant to stick to the facts in getting to the truth. Would that be possible?

I could readily understand there is no such thing as universal scientific truth. All established scientific findings remain facts in their entirety. Indeed, facts and truths are not the same. Truth would be truth forever, but a fact is true for now, not necessarily true permanently. Even at the time, in my humble opinion, scientific knowledge taught to our students was scientific facts not necessarily true forever. Notwithstanding, they would be handy and useful for the time and space we were in then. That mattered more in educating our present generation. Knowledge we were dishing out in our courses was not relative to the sense and perception of any religion of our students. For a start, I couldn't find a shred of information to add Islamic contents to my microbiology and immunology lectures. It never occurred to me at all when looking at the bacteria or culturing the viruses in the labs that there was anything Islamic about them.

It was truly a challenging time for me as the dean of a faculty where our student enrolment was not only Malays but also Kadazans, Dusuns, Muruts, Chinese, and Indians practicing different religions. I was adamant that to inculcate only Islamic perspectives in all science courses offered to our students of varying religions would be wrong. Period! A strong stand for me to stick to but not necessarily without any backlash from my immediate bosses then. I simply didn't have a clue how to play my cards right without being labelled anti-Islam. A stressful time indeed.

Today, fossil evidence seem to suggest that humans and the great apes of Africa including chimpanzees and bonobos share a common ancestor that lived between 8 million and 6 million years ago. Human evolution indeed involves a lengthy process of change. I have been met with blank bewildered stares from people when I tried to explain how this evolutionary process works and the length of time it has been going on. To make my point across, I usually resorted to a fun calculation I once came across. That seemed to help a little. Our planet Earth is about 4.5 billion years old. However, life did not exist on this planet until 3.5 billion to 4 billion years ago. The first life forms were very basic when certain kinds of bacteria and algae began to appear. This allowed for the evolution of more complex life forms. The first multicellular organisms did not appear until about 610 million years ago. Earth's biodiversity increased more rapidly when plants started to colonise the land about 430 million years ago. Then came the reptiles 300 million years ago. Dinosaurs were in the reptile group, which also included turtles, crocodiles, birds, lizards, and snakes. But 66 million years ago, towards the end of the Mesozoic Era, there was a dramatic event that led to the mass extinction of species on Earth. An estimated 70 per cent of plant and animal species perished. All of the dinosaurs went extinct. Many other reptiles survived, however, which eventually gave rise to modern reptiles.

Modern mammals arrived 75 million years ago. The human ancestors were the synapsid reptiles that lived during the Permian and Triassic periods 250 million years ago. They displayed a number of mammalian characteristics. They were not lizard men who morphed into human, but these lizards gradually evolved into mammals that eventually evolved into us, humans. The first apes appeared about 35 million years ago, and the first apelike men came about 10 million years ago. Ancestors of modern man have been on Earth for only about 3 million years. So if the 4.5-billion-year history of the Earth were to be measured in proportion to one year, man did not appear on planet Earth until December 31, at 8:30 in the evening! A lot of things have been happening here on Earth before we came into the picture. We have just been here in an infinitesimal stretch of time. Most humbling indeed!

Modern humans *Homo sapiens* started evolving in Africa around 2 million years ago before leaving the continent and migrating across the world. Fossil evidence suggested they reached the Indonesian island of Java more than 1.5 million years ago. Within the past 200,000 years , the first known human species to leave Africa, *Homo erectus,* which means 'upright man' was able to go about on two legs and use tools for hunting animals for food.

And yet within that incredibly miniscule period, the evolution of modern humans from our hominid ancestor is said to occur in four major phases. Firstly, terrestriality, meaning our ability to successfully live on land; secondly, bipedalism, meaning ability to move by means of our two rear limbs or legs; thirdly, encephalisation, meaning our possession of a large brain; and, fourthly, civilisation, the most advance stage of evolution in which the animal shows social, cultural, and organisational structure. The first humans, *Homo habilis*, emerged in Eastern and Southern Africa around 2 million years ago, long before the modern humans, *Homo sapiens*, appeared on the same continent. *Homo habilis* is also known as 'handy man' because evidence suggests of their ability to chip away at rocks, sharpening them for cutting up game or scraping hides; whilst a woman, with her child, gathers wild berries to eat and use branches to make shelters.

Scientifically, a 'human' is anyone who belongs to the genus *Homo*, Latin for 'man'. Scientists still only vaguely know when or how the first humans evolved, but they have identified a few of the oldest ones. Besides *Homo habilis*, others include *Homo rudolfensis*, who lived in Eastern Africa about 1.9 million to 1.8 million years ago, and *Homo erectus*, the 'upright man' who ranged from Southern Africa all the way to modern-day China and Indonesia from about 1.89 million to 110,000 years ago. The oldest *Homo sapiens* fossils suggested we have been around since 315,000 years ago. DNA evidence comparing different human genomes of our close cousins like Neanderthals and Denisovans seemed to show a split between the three groups at least 400,000 years ago. So it's possible that *H. sapiens* is over half a million years old.

Homo habilis known as the 'handy man' emerged about 1.8 million years ago, had a larger brain than earlier human ancestors reflected in significant changes to the shape of the skull. By then, not much had changed in their other features, including limb proportions and their hairy body, compared to those of the earlier australopithecine ancestors.

We look forward to learning more about our origin and evolution from the information contained in our DNA. It is our blueprint of life. It's a humongous source of information compactly contained in an invisibly small nuclei of our cells. The entire DNA is, however, of reasonable length. Jeremy Narby has calculated some amazing numbers in relation to this intelligent DNA. If the DNA packed into the invisibly small nuclei of each of our cells were stretched out, it would be about six inches long. End to end, the DNA of our several trillion cells would extend so far that it would take a jet plane travelling 1,000 kilometres per hour over two centuries to reach its end. Mind-boggling indeed!

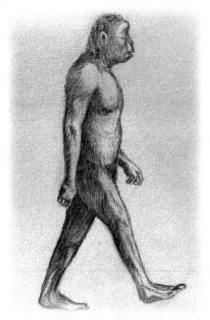

Bipedalism, ability to walk upright using two feet , brought many advantages to the future of hominid species. The trait allowed them to completely free their arms, enabling them to invent and use tools efficiently, reach for fruits in trees and use their hands for communication and social exhibits.

So when did we evolve from monkeys? But let us understand where monkeys came from first. Old World monkeys evolved from prosimians, the group of primates that included the lorises, galagos, and tarsiers. This took place during the Eocene Epoch around 50 million years ago. Then 33 million to 34 million years ago, apes evolved from these early catarrhines in Africa to later catarrhines, which include gibbons, orangutans, gorillas, chimpanzees, and humans. Amongst them, the Aegyptopithecus is considered a likely contender for the common ancestor of modern-day catarrhines. This is also assumed to be the earliest possible divergence that took place leading to the split lineages of the Old World monkeys and our more immediate ancestors the hominoids. Apes today are divided into the lesser apes and the greater apes. Humans are one type of several living species of great apes. Fossil evidence amply suggested we have evolved alongside orangutans, chimpanzees, bonobos, and gorillas. With them we share a common ancestor about 7 million years ago.

Slow Loris represent one of the prosimians, the earlier ancestors of primates. It possesses big toes on its hind feet to give this nocturnal animal gripping power.

The Common Tree Shrew , another prosimian primate, believed to represent the bridge between early terrestrial mammals and the first prosimians. It spends most of its solitary life on or close to the ground.

Tree-hugging nocturnal prosimian, the Tarsier is the only primate able to rotate its head through 180 degrees. Other primates only manage to perform a 90 degree turn maximum.

The origin of higher primates, including us, is a contentious subject amongst scientists. A series of fossils found in Egypt led to the commonly held belief that Africa was our original home. Recent discoveries, however, have suggested that we might have actually originated from Asia. One thing that has consistently baffled researchers is how our common ancestors arrived in different parts of the world ranging from Africa to South America. Numerous ideas of this happening during the continental drift and plate tectonics have been looked at. The phenomenon has become a catch-all explanation for many of the primate species distributions. For the monkeys, for instance, the explanation is quite straightforward. In the distant past, Africa and South America formed part of a much larger land mass called Gondwana. There was no Atlantic Ocean separating the present two great continents. So the primitive ancestors of Old World and New World monkeys could have literally walked or swung to what is now South America's east coast. Latest evidence seems to also suggest the ancestors of modern South American monkeys such as the capuchin and woolly monkeys first came to the New World by floating across the Atlantic Ocean on mats of vegetation and earth. The working hypothesis is that monkeys living from Africa were swept up in intense storms and found themselves at sea. They would be clinging to storm debris that formed natural rafts, and ocean currents carried these platforms of vegetation across to South America. Back then, during a time known as the late Eocene, Africa and South America were significantly closer. The span of the Atlantic Ocean between the two continents measured about 930 to 1,300 miles apart compared to the modern expanse of 1,770 miles. Upon arrival in a new continent, the surviving monkeys found a suitable new home and began to proliferate. This puts the story about the hairless Christopher Columbus discovering America pale in comparison. Our seafaring monkeys deserve their own place in history.

Since billions of years, evolution hadn't stopped. It kept on creating species after species by the trillions through adaptation and natural selection as predicted by Charles Darwin and Alfred Wallace. Today, there are monkeys and apes. Monkeys diverged into two separate lineages: one of these lineages ultimately evolved into gorillas and chimps, and the other evolved into early human ancestors called hominids. As discussed above, one of the earliest known humans is *Homo habilis*, or 'handy man', who lived about 2.4 million to 1.4 million years ago in Eastern and Southern Africa. Although we can't recognise this difference on sight, apes have an appendix organ and monkeys do not. Interestingly, the function of this appendix that sits in the lower right abdomen is unclear. One theory is that the appendix acts as a storehouse for good bacteria important in our digestive system. But experts believe the appendix is just a useless remnant from our evolutionary past.

Apes are generally more intelligent than monkeys, and most species of apes exhibit some use of tools. They have lost their tails as a consequence of natural selection. The presence of a tail, even if only a tiny nub, distinguishes monkeys from apes. Most monkeys have a short, relatively flat face without great prominence of the muzzle, although baboons and mandrills are notable exceptions. Apes and monkeys have large brains and are known for their inquisitiveness and intelligence. Brain development, combined with the freeing of the hands and well-developed vision, allows them a great latitude of activity. Most are good at solving complex problems and learning from experience. Monkeys, however, do not quite reach the cognitive levels of great apes. In strong contrast to the great apes (gorillas, chimpanzees, and orangutans), most monkeys do not appear to be very good at learning from each other's experience. Monkeys as individuals would generally learn new behaviours for themselves, not for others.

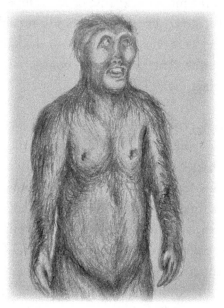

Human has mostly naked skin. Loss of fur was an adaptation to cool the body under the glaring sun when our early ancestors took to hunting animals. They travelled longer distances into the plains and other more exposed regions where wildlife was plentiful.

Monkeys are grouped into two: the Old World and the New World monkeys. Biological taxonomists use 'New World' label for groups of species found exclusively in the Americas, and 'Old World' species in Europe, Africa, and Asia. Old World and New World monkey species have evolved quite separately, which happens almost at the same time some 45 million to 35 million years ago during the late Eocene and early Oligocene periods. Today, all monkeys share many anatomical and behavioural characteristics, suggesting they have evolved from a common ancestry, the prosimian group. The fact that there are no apes in the New World suggests that they evolved quite separately. This is called parallel evolution. The complete division between New World and Old World monkeys is thought to have completed about 30 million years ago.

Unlike their Old World counterparts, New World monkeys are confined almost exclusively to a life on treetops. They have unique prehensile tails, which serves as the fifth limb. With it, the animal is equipped with the extra ability to grasp branches, fruits, and leaves within reach on the treetops. This prehensile tail makes them highly adaptable to a life above the forest floor travelling from tree to tree feeding entirely on leaves and fruits.

The Old World monkeys are not confined to life on the trees. Unlike their strictly arboreal cousins of the New World, they face more competitions for food. They have to seek and compete with other animals of the forest for food. They must include other types of food in their diet other than leaves and fruits found on the treetops. To successfully compete, their body sizes need to increase. They need to be stronger, bigger, and more adaptable than the New World monkeys, which are generally quite small weighing less than ten kilograms. The Old World monkeys range from fifteen to twenty kilograms in weight.

They are faced with more predators away from the treetops. Their daily predators are not limited to large pythons and birds of prey but also ferocious leopards and tigers of the rainforests. The males of the Old World monkeys have to become more aggressive unlike the New World monkeys. In the canopy, dews formed on the leaf tips can no longer provide water in the quantity required for normal functioning of their large body sizes. To be more successful, the monkeys of the Old World found throughout the forests of Europe, Africa, and Asia are forced to return to the ground for food and water.

About 35 million years ago, monkeys, like the baboons and macaques, have adapted well to survive on the ground in addition to their life on treetops. They have evolved to develop powerful means to keep predators on the ground at bay. As a result, they become big and ferocious. They travel in groups to be safer. This way, they do not become prey as easily to hungry terrestrial predators prowling on the forest floor.

Today, the Old World monkeys are divided into two distinct groups. The first group consists the guenons, the mangabeys, the baboons, and the macaques. They all spend some time on the ground. They are predominantly omnivorous, eating leaves, fruits, and other parts of the plants whilst readily supplementing their diet with insects, small birds, mammals, and lizards.

This group of Old World monkeys has evolved to have special cheek pouches in which they store food as they feed. This guarantees they will have enough food reserved if they have to suddenly escape from predators or involve in a fight with others clamouring for the same food source.

The second group is the colobus monkeys and the langurs. They are by and large leaf eaters. This also means they must evolve to have a means of breaking down the tough cellulose found in the leaves. Leaf monkeys, therefore, have evolved to develop a special stomach to help digest cellulose as much as possible. They do not have cheek pouches. Perhaps they don't need to because there are ample leaves to live on in the canopy and few predators to flee from when feeding.

There are also anatomical features that seem to be different in New World and Old World monkeys. Old World monkeys have nostrils that are close together, facing downwards and outwards. This facial characteristic differs from the New World monkeys. Another obvious difference in the position of their thumbs. The thumbs of Old World monkeys are fully opposable. This allows them to grab things better. Hence, there is no need for prehensile tail. Because they spend longer times on their bottoms sitting and feeding, Old World monkeys have hard pads known as ischial callosities. This acts as cushions keeping their bottoms comfortable as they rest or feed on branches or on the ground. They don't have to feed on the run all the time because they are quite safe and uninterrupted by competitors or predators around.

Homo habilis, also known as "handy man" is a forerunner of *Homo sapiens.* They were first to evolve fully opposable thumbs enabling them to grip and use weapons for hunting.

The reason other primate**s** aren't evolving into humans is that they're doing just fine. There are so many more ants in the world than humans, and they were well adapted to where they were living at the time. So evolution can happen by different mechanisms like natural selection and genetic drift. As our environment is always changing, natural selection is always happening. Humans are still evolving. But another variant or new species of ourselves is unlikely to change in our lifetime.

Extinction is forever but evolution is still happening. Man's sophisticated means of communication, locomotion. sense of seeing, hearing, smell and cognition shall be passed to generations after us to last many hundreds of million years more.

Evidence accumulating thus show Old World monkeys sharing some key characteristics with the apes and man. Humans and the Old World monkeys have evolved to share features inherited from our early ancestors. For instance, we have similar noses and the same arrangement of teeth and possess communal or social living habits.

We have the ability to adapt successfully to different climatic and environmental conditions.

Compared to other primates, humans are practically bald, and this may have allowed our species to thrive. We have evolved to be a naked ape despite fur being beneficial for our ancestors to insulate and protect the skin. What gives? Hominins, our extinct ancestors, have fur to keep them warm on cold nights. But since able to walk upright and have a slightly bigger brain, our hunting ancestors Hominids started to travel far and wide for food. Open savannahs where there were more wildlife to eat became their hunting grounds. But their fur-covered skin was making them too hot to be moving about hunting in the open all day under the glaring heat of the sun. Furthermore, their fur became a hinderance during running and chasing after animals to satisfy their newly acquired taste for meat. They soon adapted to run long distances and spend longer time hunting. They could only keep going if they were able to lose excess body heat. Losing body hair was one way. Their ability to sweat also became important to prevent overheating. Today there are no other primates that sweat more than humans. We have evolved to possess the most number of sweat glands; in excess of five millions capable of secreting as much as 12 litres of sweat per day. We lost our heavy coat of hair and gained more sweat glands probably at about the same time.

These are some of the evidence underpinning our belief that Old World monkeys form an important connection to our past. I want to share my world with my distant cousins in the primate world. My thoughts are always about associating myself with what their natural world is all about and has to offer. I crave to understand more about the species of monkeys and apes around me. They are the closest creatures to humans. I have always held a soft spot with monkeys and apes. I spent a major part of my academic career doing research in microbiology and immunology. Each experiment I carried out in the lab would normally aim as applying the results of my investigations to human diseases. At the back of my mind, I have always toyed with the idea of one day testing the science I discovered in the lab in a laboratory animal. Primates are so closely related to humans genetically. It is only logical to eventually test my findings in experimental models that are most closely related to man. Monkeys have been contributing immensely as the base of scientific research in evolution and animal communication. In the medical fields, they have been pivotal in the countless discoveries that have expanded our understanding of our own body. They have also served as indispensable models in our search for vaccines and medicinal drugs in the prevention of diseases. Perhaps monkey and apes are there to save the human race from extinction in playing that fateful and sinister role. I have been putting a lot in my working life as a sideline environmentalist and conservationist to protect them. I have devoted much time and efforts to saving their rainforest habitats. My priority is to protect, not destroy nature. Nature's ways and wisdom keep growing on me and subconsciously have become my own nature in dealing with things in my life. In the ensuing chapters, I present my blossoming affinity and kinship with monkeys and apes. Over the years, I have observed them in the wild often enough to etch in my mind the endearments and fascinations I have towards these minions of the rainforests. The narratives are drawn from my secondary readings and experiential encounters I can still vividly recall years into my retirement. My precious moments with monkeys and apes have been both a humbling reflection of eternal bliss as well as nagging concerns for their future.

ALL PLAY AND TOIL MAKES
MACAQUE A MERE JOY

SPARKLING LIKE A LITTLE GEM within the expanse of deep blue ocean lies the fascinating Pulau Tiga. A mere 300 kilometres northwest of Kota Kinabalu, Sabah, this idyllic island of about 600 hectares, stands secluded off the coast of Kimanis Bay. It keeps hordes of underwater secrets waiting to be discovered. I did my first open-water scuba dive here way back in 1983 when a team of marine scientists from the now defunct Universiti Kebangsaan Malaysia, Sabah Campus (UKMS) was tasked to document the richness and diversity of corals reefs here. The Sabah government was keen to assess the tourism potentials of the island as a scuba diving destination. The director of Taman Sabah, Datuk Lamri Ali engaged our team at UKM Sabah to inventorise the diversity of corals and associated communities of the reefs there. We were most intrigued by what we saw. Despite its remote location, this little gem did indeed possess what it took to become one of the world's top diving haven. It had a lot to offer in terms of richness and diversity of tropical marine life. At the time, I was still a novice open-water diver. Understandably, I thought the coral reefs of Pulau Tiga were in a class of their own with respect to marine biodiversity. It could indeed turn out as one of the premier diving destinations in the region.

Streaks of light began to penetrate the morning sky. Dawn was but a thin layer of lighter painted backdrop on the eastern horizon. Except for a few terns signalling to their chicks of the impending morning, much of life here were still in their slumber. I felt the morning peace and tranquillity almost maddening. As the island reverberated with shrills of terns and boobies, the island remained a symbol of unspoilt beauty and wilderness for generations. The sun had climbed to not quite directly overhead. The morning tide was fast ebbing. I almost could visualise the speed of waterline receding towards the horizon.

Long-tailed macaque is the most successful primate to have adapted and lived amongst the human environment. It has even acquired novel communication with humans using vocalisation and gestures to ask for food by extending their hand with an open palm towards us.

The entire mid-morning was at my mercy to kill. I decided to start exploring the long stretch of shady mudflats close to the estuary. That would take me till lunchtime when the rest of the team were up to start the survey of the coral reefs. Carefully placing my bare feet on patches of drying mud, I moved aimlessly towards the east side of the island where I was greeted by a rocky shore rich in barnacles and a variety of shellfish. The littoral zone had always fascinated me. A non-contiguous array of strange sea creatures, especially bivalves, crabs, and other shellfish, evolved and adapted to survive in this constantly advancing and ebbing zones. I stopped to bend over, squatting on the sandy shore to pick up anything worthy of curiosity. Broken shells of bivalves littered the sandy shore. They had been prised open and feasted by seabirds. I scrutinised floating debris of mangrove fruits and flowers that must have originated from a healthy stretch of mangroves in the proximity. I stepped further towards the sea to rinse my sandy fingers in puddles of seawater trapped between small boulders on the beach. Indifferently, I picked up a twig and poked into holes I saw in the sand, half expecting some frightened creatures might just scuttle up to the surface and challenge me, the human intruder.

In the beginning, long pointy canines in primates evolved not for tearing and ripping meat. Our ancestors used them as weapons to fight male rivals for mating rights. Over time, we increasingly have smaller canines as we stopped using teeth as weapons.

My eyes suddenly caught sight of blurry silhouettes of long-tailed creatures not far out at sea amongst the rocks half submersed in the ebbing tide. My leisurely stroll came to an abrupt halt as I strained my eyes to make out what I was seeing. They were long-tailed macaque (*Macaca fascicularis*) way out at sea. A troop of about eight individuals were busy feeding. They were knocking hard on the rocks exposed during the low tide using one hand and putting stuff into their mouths with the other. Through my binoculars, I deciphered they were breaking some kinds of shellfish to eat. That made sense because these monkeys were also known as crab-eating macaques.

As a kid in my little village, Jelawat, Kelantan, I've always considered these macaques pests. Not far from our house, my family had a reasonably big piece of land that my late grandfather had turned into an orchard of sort. He had planted fruit trees including a variety of tropical fruits: langsats, rambutans, durians, and jackfruits. Every fruiting season, these macaques got to harvest our rambutans before us. We only realised our fruits were ready for the picking after seeing rambutan skins littered on the ground directly underneath the trees.

As a species, long-tailed macaques are considered very successful. They have adapted well to exist alongside humans living in a wide range of environment. Today, macaques can be found in the busiest of cities as well as the wildest of jungles. They have become urbanised of sort. These creatures have become so emboldened as to sneak into people's kitchens in newly developed housing estates. They have acquired human skills equivalent to that of a human toddler. For instance, they have learned how to unscrew bottle tops, leverage open tins, and open pot lids to help themselves to human foods. Many a time, a family friend living in Taman Tun Dr Ismail would come back to find their kitchen raided by these cheeky thieves whilst they were at the office all day.

Yawning in monkeys could mean different things. It could be a signal to intimidate intruders and predators, yawning is also displayed when they are excited, in stressful mental states or even showing warm emotional feelings.

When we bought our first house in Subang Jaya in late 1970s, I used to take my five-year old daughter Azizah to a small patch of forests left untouched by the real estate developers. It was a few minutes' walk along tarred road behind our house. Azizah had seen monkeys and apes in cages at zoos we visited in the United States and Canada during my graduate studies. But she had not seen monkeys roaming free jumping around on trees or walking and skipping on the ground. Each visit there would be a real treat for her before dinner. She would be screaming full of glee and excitement wanting to get closer and closer to these creatures and feed them peanuts. She'd be looking forward to this feeding frenzy every day as soon as I got back from work at UKM located in Jalan Pantai, Kuala Lumpur, then. As she was nervously throwing the peanuts to the monkeys that came to greet us, Azizah would be shouting commands for them to share their peanuts she was generously throwing at them. 'Hey, you! You, the fat one over there, be nice. Share! These peanuts are not just for you. Share! Share!' She would get frustratingly crossed at the ones that seemed to be greedy and naughty. Some male monkeys would be hoarding the peanuts and quickly shoving them in their mouths till both sides of the cheeks bulged with food. In Azizah's little brain, that looked so disgusting and utterly unfair.

Facial expression is big in the Macaque world. They use almost all anatomical features on their face to communicate; like displaying aggressive or threatening stances through raised up eyebrows, sharp glaring eyes and opening the mouth wide to bare their ferocious set teeth.

How would a father explain such behaviour to a five-year-old child? It wasn't bullying or disgusting at all. Such seemingly greedy demeanour is one of the survival modes shaped by biological evolution and adaptation in the primate world. Monkeys have open cheek pouches within the oral cavity, which are essentially pockets between the jaw and the cheeks on both sides of the head. Cheek pouches are found in other mammals too, including the platypus, some rodents, and bats. But most monkeys have cheek pouches. Interestingly, cheek pouches are also found in marsupial koala. Because they are located on both sides of the mouth, these mammals are named *diplostomes,* meaning 'two mouths'. The size of cheek pouches vary in different animals. In some rodents such as hamsters, the pouches are remarkably developed, forming two bags that extend from the mouth to the front of the shoulders.

The sight of two oversized skin ballooning on each side of their faces whilst feeding can indeed look disgusting. Where are your table manners, mate? But that can be absolutely explicable in the monkey's world. The act of stuffing their mouths and awkwardly hogging the food in the cheek pouches is not at all a greedy or selfish behaviour as construed by humans. Cheek pouches have several roles. Whilst they allow the rapid collection of food, pouches also serve as temporary storage and transport. The hoarding of food and temporarily storing them to be consumed later have become a survival strategy in the monkey world. Not at all a selfish greedy habit. They would resort to this when they fear danger. In the presence of intruders or competitors going for the same food, cheek pouches allow them to carry their food to safer locations. It definitely appeared as if they lacked consideration for others as they escaped the chaotic scene pressing their pouches to the back of the mouth with the back of the legs and moving the jaw at the same time.

Macaques cheeks are like small deflated balloons that they gluttonously stuff with food during feeding. Hoarding food is a defence mechanism that allows them to carry food to safer locations away from competing members to be savoured in peace later.

In Nepal and Myanmar, these monkeys are sacred in temples. They are spared from any kind of harm no matter how mischievous or problematic they could be. Religious beliefs put them as reincarnated beings of past ancestors. Hence, they will be well treated, absolutely safe, and protected here. They truly live up to their reputation of cheeky monkeys. At a temple I once visited in Myanmar, these macaques were infamous for stealing items like cameras, mobile phones, sunglasses, and hats from tourists and would ask for some food in exchange for the return of stolen items. They knew too well no humans would harm them there. They would refuse returning their stolen goods until given food in exchange. They have learned that stealing is too opportunistic and slow at getting food. Instead, robbing and bartering could be the new norm. Amazing how the learned behaviour of these monkeys have evolved from using rocks to break shellfish to trading human possessions for food.

In some religions, macaques are sacred and of spiritual significance to be revered. They represent the energy surrounding the temples and therefore safe and tolerated by worshippers despite their nuisance and mischievous antics.

Their success as a species is in their omnivorous diet. Having a generalist diet, they feed on fruits, nuts, leaves, and insects. Here in the mangroves, they are always surrounded by ample supply of vegetation to feed on. During low tide, they would venture down onto the reefs and wade around in shallow waters to hunt for crabs. I have seen videos of long-tailed macaques diving down to the sea bottom looking for crabs and other edible marine life. As a group, they seem to enjoy a friendly and relaxed social structure, equally at home in the trees and on the ground.

I looked up to see the commotion coming from the beach vegetation a few metres away on my right. A troop of about half-a-dozen individuals was busy monkeying around. They didn't seem to be alarmed by my presence. Oblivious to my intrusion, the juveniles were preoccupied with sprinting and pushing each other playfully. The older ones engaged themselves lazily in mutual grooming. I had a quick flashback of myself as a kid sitting on the stairs to my village house carefully picking strands of grey hairs from my grandmother's head using a grain of paddy, rough and still in its hull. But picking greying hairs wasn't at all what these monkeys were doing! They were grooming.

Macaques spend a lot of time sitting around, poring and picking on each other's furry bodies. Mutual grooming is important in the primate world, and the practice is very much political. Widely performed between the subordinates and their superiors, grooming helps to stabilise social groups. They express affection and make peace with others by grooming each other. Grooming also seems to be a way of making peace after a fight amongst themselves. They also engage in grooming as a gesture to make friends with other troop members. Generally, grooming helps monkeys build and maintain good social relationships.

Peacekeeping

Getting accepted by their own kind and belonging to a desired group of individuals are central in the lives of social animals. Humans often go to great lengths to please their loved ones. We also resort to pandering and giving in to build friendship or gain favours from others. Macaques are social animals that have similar needs. Their way of getting accepted or befriending others is through grooming. This is when they spend a lot of time going through each other's hair, picking and eating lice or parasites they might find in there—a healthy ritual that keeps them free of harmful parasitic infections. From the social perspective, the act of grooming also serves to reinforce social bonds within the group, seek companionship, and maintain peace between different groups.

Whilst mutual grooming between individuals of similar social standing and youngsters increases bonding, the act also serves a hygienic purpose. It helps to get rid of external parasites. Intestinal helminths are often found sticking to furs contaminated with their own faeces. They will be picking carefully through each other's hair, eating any parasites they might find. The practice helps keep their fur clean of dirt, dead skin, and parasites at all times. Grooming thus serves to both keep the monkeys healthy as well as reinforce social cohesion.

Facial expressions during play and interactions are important for both social and cognitive development of young macaques. The extensive time spent on playing is related to the size of an important part of the brain responsible for learning behaviour. Play apparently facilitates learning and development.

Invariably, females do most of the grooming in the group. A devoted mother would search over most of her youngster's body, looking closely at the skin and hairs. Adult males look forward to being groomed by their subordinates, which are usually females or younger adults. They seem to idly wait for their turn. By the look of it, there must be some form of contentment or sheer pleasure derived from the act of grooming. A state of ecstasy is normally shown by those being groomed as they lie on their back, eyes half closed, and would even allow themselves to be gently shoved around in the process. The older macaques seem to show a considerable amount of patience. I found much delight in seeing such compassion and care in these creatures often regarded as pests or intruders into our space. It makes me wonder who are the intruders, us or them?

Coming from the direction I left about an hour ago, I could hear human voices carried by the westerly winds along the shore. The rest of the research team were already up getting ready for their first dive of the day. I decided to kill a little more time on my own as the morning sun gradually set the entire seascape aglow. It felt good to subconsciously sink my feet in the soft sand as I continued strolling along. The warm sea foams surged with the ebbing tide, gently touching and drenching my heels and toes. Against the shimmering glare of the noon sun, a solitary green heron (*Butorides striatus*) was foraging on the open mudflats. This is quite a treat! Green herons usually hunt from cover. Rarely do they hunt openly on mudflats like this, I thought.

I was startled by another commotion within the mangroves on my right. I counted the troop was made up of seven to ten individuals. Long-tailed macaques are known to live in groups of both sexes and all ages. They hardly travel on their own. They do this for safety. In the rainforests, macaques' main predators include the leopard cats and pythons. In any group, one dominant male will take charge. I spotted a dominant male strutting almost arrogantly on a vantage point of the highest tree branch overlooking others. He moved around with his head held high. There was an atmosphere of supreme authority about every step he took— enough to tell potential rival males to stay absolutely clear of any trouble. Occasionally, long-tailed macaques would join forces to form temporary groups of up to more than 100 animals. This could be a strategy of strength in numbers offering strong resistance to potential predators.

The atmosphere was unsettlingly boisterous and raucous. Some adult monkeys were bouncing and jumping, rowdily letting out forceful vocal sounds. A large alpha monkey turned to face me and contorted a series of threatening facial expressions. He was communicating with me, I figured. He was warning me from approaching his domain, essentially saying, 'Stay out, this is my territory.' I heeded with no argument whatsoever. I stopped short on my track, stepped back, and continued to study their behaviour.

Macaques employ facial expressions to convey their intentions to rival males and to potential mates. A yawn, for instance, is not to be taken as just a typical harmless gesture. Yawning of one male to another could be a full threat alert, the ultimate last warning display of sort. A sharp stare could also be a threat. So be careful. Confronting these variable facial expressions, members of the group would learn to gauge the degree and seriousness of the threats. Within the groups, this threatening display can be a gesture of dominance from one male to another to stay away. Other males nearby would respond accordingly by looking down almost sheepishly. Without ado, he would move away from the dominant male. This way they avoid disturbing the peace of others around by avoiding fights amongst them. The youngsters, too, recognise and act obediently to such gestures. By submitting to commands and warnings of the dominant males, respect and harmony within the group would be maintained. Each macaque, regardless of social status, could then go about their own business.

On occasions, macaques could be fighting and defending themselves from predators or other headstrong males. Under such circumstances, macaques would wilfully and energetically bite. This, too, is usually pre-empted by specific facial gestures. They might put on a huge grin or pull and stretch their lips to show their ferocious set of canines. It might seem like a smile to us. Believe me, in the monkey world, this could be a sign of aggression or anger. Again, the words of Wak Moh, the Jelawat beruk trainer during my childhood days, came flashing in my head. He had always repeatedly warned us kids to not treat the many gestures made by his beruk as mere bluffs. Head bobbing, yawning, grinning to expose the teeth, and jerking his head and shoulders back and forth could well be signs of aggression that we kids must learn to respect at all times.

The mood above on the tree branches within the canopy was not all violent and aggressive. There was an exuberance of fun and games too. Slapping each other on the head, followed by chasing, swinging, climbing, and rolling over one another were all in the spirit of play. The young ones seemed forever interested in just fooling around and amusing themselves. Play in animals has always been something of an enigma to those studying animal behaviour. Young animals of primate species seem to enjoy playing, but the purpose is not immediately clear. The mother seemed to just sit there giving a close watch. At times, her face lighted up in glee. Animal behaviour experts believe playing constitute a crucially important phase of development in the monkey world. It is a process by which they acquire skills they would one day need as adults.

Standing there totally enjoying the goings-on, I was not fully convinced about this purposive nature of playing around in the primate world. I couldn't help noticing the sparks in their eyes and body language amidst all those monkeying around. I found it strikingly fascinating the juveniles seemed to be playing the fool a lot just like our children growing up. It clearly gave me the impression the juveniles especially were just simply having fun. They might not feel the emotions in the same way as we humans seek to enjoy, but I could swear they show signs and gestures of excitement, glee, and pleasure. It seems most obvious that happiness and joy are emotions not solely displayed by humans. It would be presumptuous, or even outright erroneous, to suggest monkeys feel emotions in the same way as our children experience during play. I would submit their playing around could benefit them socially like bonding or making peace amongst them. But those social outcome eventuate subconsciously, not on purpose. Notwithstanding, my close observations of these primates at play unquestionably suggest happiness as the end, not the means. They play for the sake of playing. Their expressions and reactions are associated with pleasure akin to those experienced by humans. Contentious or not, that makes me jump to my own conclusion—happiness and joy are emotions not exclusively that of humans, but monkeys too. Anyone who has ever watched young monkeys at play would definitely nod in agreement with me.

Macaca fascicularis is one of the most geographically widespread non-human primate species in the world. They are commonly found living within the peripheries or buffer zones between the rainforests and human settlements. Their ability to adapt, survive, and breed successfully amidst our modern environment is just remarkable. Unfortunately, long-tailed macaques are increasingly looked upon as nuisance and pests because of their rapid encroachment into our living space, our orchards, our temples, and even our cities. Could this be an equivalent retaliation to our decades of clearing the mangroves and rainforests that used to be their domain, not ours? A tit for tat, if you will. Their new disrepute as trouble in our midst has prompted many studies on the behaviour, social organisation, habitat usage, morphology, and genetics of long-tailed macaques.

Currently, long-tailed macaques are categorised as 'least concern' on the IUCN Red List. At the same time, the species is also often classified as 'widespread, and rapidly declining'. Obviously this is because there is no conservation efforts dedicated to protecting this highly adaptable monkey. Instead, trade of long-tailed macaques for biomedical research has increased significantly in recent years. This despite the species' inclusion in CITES appendix 2, which requires regulation of wildlife trade internationally. In Southeast Asian countries, macaques are not protected and national wildlife trade is not regulated.

Being highly adaptable around human, long-tailed macaques have become a hardy species. It also thrived well in captivity. Because of this, they have found themselves in laboratories used in scientific research. Furthermore, monkeys are genetically and biologically close to man. Hence, they are used extensively in medical and physiological research. There have been notable contributions to medical research from use of macaques. This include the discovery of Rh factor from rhesus monkeys. Arguably, this has been the most important discovery that has saved many lives. Rh factors is a genetically determined protein found on the surface of red blood cells. Not everyone has this rare protein termed as being Rh-positive. A huge proportion of people are Rh-negative. If the blood of an Rh-positive mother mixed with the blood of her Rh-negative baby at birth, problems may arise. During pregnancy, the antibodies from the mother's blood may cross the placenta to fight the Rh-positive red blood cells of the baby. This can prove fatal to unborn or newly born infant. Such unfortunate circumstance is especially manifested during the mother's second pregnancy. Landmark contributions in using macaques for medical research were also in the area of disease prevention. For instance, the polio vaccine, which had saved millions of lives, was first developed in crab-eating macaques.

Long-tailed macaques have long become the experimental "guinea pigs" for scientific research. Their immune and nervous systems are very similar to humans, making them suitable research 'models' for a range of investigations including neurological disorders such as Parkinson's disease, reproduction. Vision and the production of vaccines.

I hurriedly walked back to join the rest of the team, who by now were getting ready for their first dive. I have dived here a few times previously. It was on this stretch of coral reefs opposite the UKMS Marine Research Station where I encountered one of the most fascinating mating rituals amongst marine animals. Besides Malaysia, I have dived in many parts of the world including Australia, Fiji, Japan, Maldives, Indonesia, Thailand, and the Philippines, but never have I seen a similar phenomenon anywhere else. Here on Pulau Tiga reefs, I bear witness to a pair of the blacktip sharks *Carcharhinus melanopterus* mating. Indeed, the textbook description of how a receptive female behaves before mating is dead accurate. The female would almost dance gracefully on the sea floor. She would swim slowly in a repetitive oscillation pattern similar to sinusoidal wave near the bottom of the sea. She would hold her head pointed down, giving the impression she was self-conscious and shy. It was amazing and bizarre at the same time. A sight to die for.

Each time, I've been most intrigued by the richness of Pulau Tiga coral reefs in terms of number and diversity of species. The reefs of Pulau Tiga were indeed a symbol of unblemished beauty of marine life in the early 1980s. I found myself marvelling at the electrifying hues and bizarre forms of marine biodiversity before me. A cast of millions resided here, marking their respective nooks and corners of habitation. A kaleidoscope of colours from dull rusty brown to iridescent green and red was simply surreal, almost mystical, further enhanced by the sunlight from above. The reefs here were a splendid representation of primarily healthy hard corals. Stunning gigantic colonies of staghorn, tabletop, and brain corals were widely distributed across the sea floor. The reefs were also home to a great variety of marine life including turtles, triggerfish, groupers, barracudas, and manta rays. I spotted a bright-orange thingy very slowly making its way out of a rocky fissure. I casually swam towards the apparently lethargic organism looking like a discarded plastic toy from a distance. It was a starfish. I picked it up and turned the creature upside down for a closer examination. It revealed hundreds of sucker-like feet. Stuck to these wiggly appendages was a pair of empty mussel shells. It has already killed and made a meal of a mussel, I matter-of-factly comprehended. This was done by employing a sophisticated internal hydraulic system assisted by its hundreds of sucker-like feet. A starfish is capable of grabbing the shells of bivalves like mussels and producing a force strong enough to pry shells apart.

It would then turn its own stomach inside out through its mouth, digest the fleshy part of the shellfish, and pull its stomach back inside when done with the meal. This creature is in fact a top predator in this underworld world. Despite lacking anything as evolved as a brain, starfish on a coral reef is like a tiger in the rainforest—a marauder capable of killing any other creatures on its path. But I still wonder why we keep referring to this creature a starfish instead of accurately calling it a sea star. Technically speaking, a starfish is no more a fish than it is an elephant.

Sea stars or starfish exhibits bizarre feeding behaviour. It wraps its body around the prey like bivalves, pulls the shells apart using suction force created by its tube feet. Succeeding, it would then pull its stomach out of its body and lunge it into the opened bivalve where digestive enzymes are secreted. After a good feed of its liquefied meal, starfish would retract its stomach back inside.

It was quarter past midnight; my body was absolutely washed out and spent. My muscles were sore with every movement of my limbs. The research team had been diving here for the full ten days in an attempt to inventorise the richness of Pulau Tiga coral reefs and their associated marine life. Tomorrow would be the last day of the entire expedition. The long list of observations and data entries would be duly analysed and documented on campus. From the casual discussions I've been following amongst the participants, many had said their initial gauge of the marine life communities here exceeded all expectations. That was most reassuring with respect to the pristine state of the coral reefs here. They appeared to have been effectively protected and managed by Sabah Parks since Pulau Tiga was declared a protected area.

After dinner, a few of us decided to walk up to the end of the jetty extending about fifty metres into the sea. Everyone felt we should go there to serenade the night away to mark the success of our expedition. The night sky was clear with the full silvery moon casting shimmering lights onto the surface of the sea. A surreal panorama of calmness I could almost picture and still feel now after almost forty years ago. Two amongst us brought along their acoustic guitars and strummed away almost as soft and rhythmic as the waves endlessly crashing along the beach. A chorus of familiar Malay and English songs filled the air. Some surprised us with incredibly perfect renditions of the evergreen songs the likes of P Ramlee, Jeffry Din, Tom Jones, and Engelbert Humperdinck. Everyone was having a ball. A great respite bathing in the moonlit night with their legs restfully dangling off the jetty. I found myself staring at the gorgeous silvery moon in the dark cloudless sky above. Because of low level of light pollution, this island has great conditions for stargazing. At certain times of the year, a keen stargazer might be able to see the five familiar constellations of the equatorial belt: Pisces, Cetus, Taurus, Eridanus, and Orion. Indeed, stargazing at Pulau Tiga could be a breathtakingly magical experience. Here, the heavens appear closer to Earth. A shooting star skipped through the dark sky. Just as suddenly, a flash of memory crossed my mind. A macaque was also a star in human's space exploration once! The first monkey to be launched into space was a male rhesus monkey named Albert II. He was successfully sent into space to a height of 134 kilometres on 14 June 1949. It was an attempt to study the physiological effects of spaceflight. Back in that era, we knew next to nothing about space medicine. What would be the physiological effects of our astronauts in space? Of interest in particular were the effects on cardiovascular systems under microgravity environment. Little was known about the results of that historic experiment because Albert died of suffocation during his flight. I began to question the wisdom of our playing tit for tat game with the macaques. They are increasingly becoming a menace encroaching into our space. Do we just tolerate this and make no effort in saving their dwindling numbers in the wild? Their genetically and biologically closeness to us can potentially lead us into unravelling much insights about the health and well-being of humanity. Their indispensable contributions in medical research have saved lives of many children and adults. With the looming possibility of our venturing more and more into the expanse beyond planet Earth, humanity will be space travellers one day. We need to do research on the short- and long-term stay in outer atmosphere before space industry becomes a dream come true. We need to experiment with species closely related to human. Other species of monkeys and apes are already on the list of threatened or critically endangered list. We just might be pushed to rely on the availability of macaques that have become to be most successful species related to man.

THE VILLAGE COCONUT PLUCKER

IN OPTING FOR ECONOMIC DEVELOPMENT, Malaysians have been most judicious. We do not usually go overboard. We have always demonstrated our love and concern for the natural environment. In my years of experience promoting ecotourism in Sabah, I have always reminded the people there not to kill the proverbial goose that lay the golden eggs. We need to be forever mindful of any potentially adverse effects of tourism activities on our ecosystems and their indigenous flora and fauna; the very raison d'être why tourists from across the globe came in droves to our country. Every development of tourism infrastructure needs to be carefully weighed out with preservation of our local and unique tourism assets in mind. So when I heard of an environmental disaster that had occurred at Tasik Chini a few years back, I was naturally curious.

I have heard so much about this hidden gem that has increasingly become a magnet for nature lovers and discerning shutterbugs. 'It only rewards people who trouble to seek it out,' I was urged by Rahmah, the deputy vice chancellor for research, UKM, who was leading a team of UKM scientists to Tasik Chini, where the university had established a research station for its students and staff. Setting off from Kuantan, about sixty kilometres away from our final destination, we passed through a long meandering stretch of oil palm plantation roads. Endless monotonous rows of oil palms provided the cooling shades much needed all along our journey. Using the rudimentary physics at my fingertips, I had anticipated a journey of about ninety minutes at the speed and distance we had to negotiate along those narrow meandering roads.

I jolted awake to realise I have been snoozing in the passenger's seat. An awe-inspiring expanse of emerald-green water greeted us upon arrival. Against a backdrop of multilayered shades of green tropical mountains, the lake glittered in the mid-morning sun. I immediately felt the peace and tranquillity often associated with the sheer vastness and panoramic landscape of a tropical freshwater lake setting. After tucking in a good lunch at the inn's restaurant, we had our first boat trip out through channels of waterways leading to the middle of the lake.

Our boatman slowly stalled the boat to give our amateur photographers a field day clicking away like there was no tomorrow. From any vantage point, the panoramic views of Tasik Chini were simply stunning. The clear reflections from its smooth water surfaces were heart-stopping. Simply out of this world. As some of us were busy fidgeting and focusing on our cameras and iPhones, one of our students spotted a couple of monkeys near the water's edge about 150 metres away. As we approached closer, it was identified as a pair of pig-tailed Macaque, *Macaca nemestrina*. That wasn't at all unexpected because we have been told about the forests surrounding the lake harbouring a variety of wildlife species. Encounters with forest primates such as the banded langur, *Presbytis femoralis;* white-handed gibbon, *Hylobates lar;* long-tailed macaque, *Macaca fascicularis;* and the Sunda pig-tailed macaque, *Macaca nemestrina,* were common.

Furthermore, the southern pig-tailed macaques are commonly kept as pets by the Jakun people, an Orang Asli tribe that still lives in a few small settlements within the proximity of the lake. They are medium-sized macaques that are found in both primary and secondary forests of southern Thailand, Malaysia, and Indonesia. Locally it is known as the beruk. Generally of larger size than the ubiquitous long-tailed macaques, the males of pig-tailed macaque can weigh up to fifteen kilograms. Like long-tailed macaques, they are mostly coated with buff-brown fur. A keen pair of eyes would invariably spot the subtle difference in the furry trunks of these two macaque species. The pig-tailed macaques present a darker dorsal area and lighter ventral area. In other words, they have a lighter-coloured underside than on their back. Their most distinguishing feature is probably their short, thick tail for which they are named, which invariably arches over their back, curling up half erect resembling the tail of a pig.

Pig-tailed macaques, gifted and skilful climbers, are being kept chained, abusively trained and forced to climb trees to pick coconuts in many parts of Southeast Asian. In the Malaysian villages, this extraordinary skill is fully exploited during Ramadan months and festive seasons when coconut juice and milk are needed for cooking traditional dishes and cakes.

Pig-tailed macaques are omnivorous, feeding primarily on fruits and seeds. They therefore need to be a highly skilled climber. In the primary rainforest, they have been observed reaching up huge towering trees in search of edible fruits. People in Asia have taken advantage of this extraordinary climbing skill for more than 400 years. In Thailand, Malaysia, and Indonesia, pig-tailed macaques have been trained to harvest coconuts.

My thoughts suddenly conjured up images of intense nostalgia. To me, growing up in a small Malay kampung, or village, was far from being inadequate or marginal. It was filled with a social memory I'll forever cherish and treasure into my old age. It has helped me to explore the connection between my social identity today and my historical past. For instance, my experiences growing up in a kampung have helped me understand why I feel so impassionedly about animals in general. One of those fond memories of growing up in my village was watching pig-tailed macaques being part and parcel of the community of Jelawat folks. I was left with an indelible mark of respect for this selfless animal. Pig-tailed macaques—the community beruk that served many families in my kampung as the coconut plucker. Coconut milk or *santan* is a must-have ingredient in a variety of Malay dishes. I used to look forward to watching pig-tailed macaques obediently following orders of his human masters. As a kid, I would tag along an elderly guy by the name of Wak Moh to get a few coconuts for my mother's kitchen. Wak Moh—I still have no idea if this was his real name—was an interesting guy, a highly reputable trainer of pig-tailed macaques, second to none. He was the man to give obedient training and discipline to this monkey species for the sole purpose of plucking coconuts. Besides Jelawat, his expertise was known even in other kampungs in the Bachok district. He was always respectful and courteous towards my parents, but strangely would invariably put on a fearsome no-nonsense kind of person for us kids. Whenever my mother wanted to cook curry or rendang, that would be the time to solicit the service of Wak Moh and his beruk. The pair would be doing brisk business during the fasting months and the eves of Hari Raya. Their exquisite services were highly in demand in the month of Ramadhan when nothing could be as thirst-quenching as the fresh coconut water for breaking fast. The coconut milk or santan squeezed from the older coconuts would be highly sought for cooking curry and rendang during the Muslim festive season Hari Raya. I marvelled at the level of communication Wak Moh had reached between him and his beruk. At his command of 'Mudo! Mudo!' only the young green coconuts would fall to the ground. Of course, that would be for the coconut water for drinking. And when the command was 'Tuo! Tuo!' the old wrinkly brown coconuts would fall, for the coconut milk or santan needed for cooking curry or rendang.

Pig-tailed macaque got its name from the curled up half-erect tail it has. From an evolutionary perspective, variations in tail length is part and parcel of mammal adaptations to achieving stability and balance during locomotion or lose heat to maintain constant body temperature

Fascinated, we would try to get closer to Wak Moh's beruk when it was done with the plucking of coconuts and returned to the ground, perhaps to congratulate or express our pleasure for a job well done. But Wak Moh would always warn us not to go too close to his beruk. We knew that too well and for a good reason too. His beruk would give a huge grin, baring all the dental armaments endowed to a primate. Those sharp pointed incisors, canines, premolars, and molars looked so potent for nipping at our arms if we got any closer. Wak Moh's beruk could easily sink his teeth in our arms and draw blood in a split second. At least that was what we thought then. Only later in life that I knew what all those grimacing and threatening gestures were all about.

They were just a threat, and that was as harmful as they got. Trained beruk very rarely made a go at humans, if at all. Most primate species, including humans, use threatening gestures and stares to intimidate others. Primatologists refer to this particular use of body language as agonistic displays. That finally took the mystery out of this bizarre behaviour of Wak Moh's beruk baring his full set of dental armaments along with his vicious facial gestures. No wonder all the years the Jelawat kids have been around Wak Moh's beruk, no one had been bitten by the gentle beast.

Pig-tailed macaque is usually solitary and peaceful. Ample warnings are issued before aggression is applied in establishing calm and social order among themselves. It can however launch a sudden offensive attack on competitors and intruders.

In the wild amongst their own groups, pig-tailed macaques seemed to enjoy all the entitlements that came with being the boss. Even then, physically violent encounters are rare amongst them. Physical aggression and fighting were only occasional and episodic. Delinquent individuals within the group were usually dealt with by the dominant male in the group. Major conflicts within the community would usually be prevented and order kept by the use of subtle agonistic displays. For instance, the dominant male would flash his eyelids when angry. This alone would intimidate others. Only when this subtle gesture wasn't sufficient in its effect would he resort to opening his mouth widely in a manner that looks like a big yawn. This is usually the last warning before attacking. This ultimate threat for others in the group would usually be heeded with things quickly returning to normal. Otherwise, pig-tailed macaques would just hang around and do little. They are not known to roam around boisterously and in big groups like the long-tailed macaques. All too often I've spotted this species forlornly sitting on their own on tree branches with chest wide open as out of breath.

Show of Strength

A show of might amongst nations competing for world dominance usually involve display of military strengths in the form of human personnel and weaponry. It's a means of wielding power to gain respect from enemies. In the macaques' world, they do this by displaying their long sharp canines, the fearsome arsenal used to intimidate and fend off intruders in the competition for dominance.

Until recently, there was uncertainty about the existence of another species of pig-tailed macaques in Southeast Asia. For some time, the species of northern pig-tailed macaque (*Macaca leonina*) was thought to be a subspecies of *Macaca nemestrina*. But now this confusion has been resolved and they are recognised as separate species. *Macaca nemestrina* found in southern Thailand, Malaysia, and Indonesia is now commonly called the southern pig-tailed macaque. Locally they are known as the beruk. Both southern and northern pig-tailed macaques have been simply referred to as 'pig-tailed macaques'.

Like other macaques, pig-tailed macaques are both terrestrial and arboreal, spending time both in the trees and on the ground. Primarily frugivorous, they thrive on fruits, which make up the majority of their diet. They are known to eat over 100 species of fruits. This points out to the crucial role they play in forest regeneration by dispersing seeds from over 100 species of plants.

Can we always interpret primates baring their teeth as a show of threat and aggression? Researchers believe such display could also be a 'tooth-baring' smile associated with friendship towards us fellow primates. We still have a lot to learn from the "culture" of our ancestral cousins.

In search of fruits, they may travel more than two kilometres a day throughout their home range. They would be exploring from tree to tree within their home range that could extend around forty-five hectares of both primary and secondary forests. Their presence in a forest area depends on the season and fruit availability. When fruits are not in season, they may resort to bird eggs and small animals such as caterpillars. Bizarrely, they are known to develop eating habits to savour even harmful caterpillars. Northern pig-tailed macaques in Thailand, for instance, have been documented to eat stinging caterpillars. But before biting and chewing away their potentially injurious morsel, they would carefully brush the stinging hairs of the caterpillars with their fingers prior to eating. They have been observed to use leaf or twigs as tools to remove the stingers.

We were sitting in a boat in the middle of the lake beneath a slightly overcast tropical sky. A cool breeze from the land soothingly wafting over the back of my neck. Encircling us were lush green forests of distant mountain ranges. The warm morning sun peeked through the clouds, casting a shimmering glow over the lake surface. It was easy to appreciate why Tasik Chini was given the status of a biosphere reserve by the world body UNESCO. Pristinely positioned amidst 12,000 acres of lush tropical rainforest, Tasik Chini is Malaysia's second-largest natural lake. The biosphere reserve is in fact twelve interconnected lakes; all of which eventually flow into Sungai Pahang. The lake features some of the most distinctive tropical ecosystems, which include the lowland rainforests, streams and rivers, wetlands, and, of course, this huge freshwater lake. I nodded instinctively whilst casting glances at the not just unique but also varied natural habitats surrounding the huge water body.

Tasik Chini's scenic value was simply top-notched, blessed with extraordinary beauty and natural resources. Celebrated primarily for its sea of lotus plants, *Nelumbo nucifera*, we were not the least disappointed with what welcomed us just minutes away from the jetty. The lotus plants were in full bloom. The expanse of the lake was just imbued with radiant white-pinkish colouration, giving Tasik Chini its picture-perfect iconic impression. It was a sight to marvel and be in awe of!

As we were busy getting good snapshots of the pair of macaques, there were movements in the lush canopy in the background. A group of monkeys emerged. Not less than six individuals seemed to join the pair we were studying previously. A reinforcement of sort. Perhaps they felt more safe and secure in numbers when faced with two boatloads of humans intruding into their natural habitat. Generally, pig-tailed macaques are not considered to be territorial. They rarely engage in conflicts with neighbouring groups at the borders of their home ranges. In fact, their home ranges often overlap extensively between different groups. But there is a hierarchy amongst the groups of pig-tailed macaques. This system in which members of the group are ranked accordingly in relation to status or authority differed in males and females. Amongst the male monkeys, the hierarchy would be based on brute and strength; whilst amongst the females, based on heredity. Thus, the daughter of the alpha female will immediately be placed above all other females to lead the group. Amongst the male monkeys, one capable of managing conflicts within the group through physical gestures and commands would be the leader of the group.

Baby macaques spend quality time with mothers that never fail to shower them with much care and appreciation for the company. Normally they do not live separately at an early age but remain in contact for at least one year till they leave and are able to fend for themselves.

This system of hierarchy dictates much of the daily life of pig-tailed macaques. Higher-ranking individuals usually have priority access to resources like food and mates. They also have priority access to females in oestrus. This is during the period the females are in heat, ready to mate with a male. Periods of oestrus signals the breeding season. The high-ranking males would often stake their 'statutory rights' by mounting aggressive behaviours to state their dominance. Other group mates would distance themselves from the females in heat. This could have driven other males to usually leave the group at sexual maturity to find a new group to integrate into. On the other hand, the high-ranking females usually stay peacefully in their birth group, forming close matrilines of mothers, daughters, sisters, and aunts. The females will give birth to a single infant after a gestation period of approximately six months. The infant will initially cling to its mother's belly before slowly becoming more independent as he or she ages.

Macaques generally are perceived as pests in orchards and crop plantations. Recently, however, the oil palm industry was told they have a friendly ally in controlling pest rodents in plantations. The Southern pig-tailed macaque, were found to devour significant numbers of rats in plantations – estimated 3,000 rats per year per macaque group. This raises the feasibility of using pig-tailed macaques as biological pest control leading to a win-win scenario in managing human-wildlife conflict in Malaysia.

Tasik Chini's immense body of fresh water is extremely important to the people living within its vicinity in terms of its water resources, ecological role, and unique fauna and flora. The lush green belt of rainforests fringing the lake is one of the most threatened habitats in the country. In a way, the plants growing here are only trees and shrubs capable of tolerating long periods of flooding. In the low-lying areas of the lakes, extensive stands of the multipurpose rasau plants, *Pandanus helicopus*, dominated the familiar landscape. The Jakun people and other local communities harvest the blades of *Pandanus* for use as roofing materials or handicrafts. The leaves are woven or plaited into mats, thatch, sails, baskets, hats, and many other items. The fruits of these rasau plants are also said to be edible. As a matter of courtesy to the indigenous people living here, we stopped at a small settlement of the Jakun community at the fringe of the forest nearby. There were close to a dozen families living in reasonably comfortable dwellings. Clearly they have been settlers at this same location for some time. It appeared they have had access to the basic government assistance in the form of clean water and an electricity generator for night use. They seemed used to having visitors dropping for a quick look around at how they thrived by this lakeside. All in all, they were a bunch of friendly lots with a good-humoured elderly chief who greeted us upon our arrival. He was extremely chatty with brilliant local tales how their ethnic tribe had been handling the problem of wild pigs plundering their plots of sweet potatoes during the night.

A strong gust seemed to blow out of thin air. Reminiscent to yesterday, the sky above looked awfully gloomy. After bidding hasty goodbyes to our hosts, we scrambled up the boat, heading back for the inn. The surface of the lake was reflecting glares of pastel-orange hues cast by the setting sun. The panoramic view was just shimmering with platinum glow, a sheer delight to feed your senses. I watched the many concentric rings of breaks rising on the lake's surface caused by fish feeding just below the surface. Swallows swooped and hit the water surface to feed on some floating larva and aquatic insects.

A low rumble of thunder was heard in the distance, threatening us with a heavy downpour. Within a few minutes, the entire sky overhead was quickly swallowed up by thick black clouds. We were just about to be drenched by a fierce tropical thunderstorm. Already, in the distant horizon, thunders and lightnings began to explode. Our boatman calmly started the outboard engine and raced back. He had to get all of us to the safety of our inn in time. The threat of a tropical shower became increasingly imminent. He decided to take a more direct route back. Adeptly, he manoeuvred the boat through small channels of waterways formed between long stretches of *Pandanus* stands. At some sharp bends, the boat stalled for more gap to sail through. We were back safe and sound within twenty minutes.

By dinner time, the thunderstorm lulled and eventually gave us a respite. I stood arm-folded on the verandah of the inn staring straight into the pitch darkness across the lake. The cool night air after the heavy downpour earlier had triggered a host of flying creatures to come out and hunt. A bat, probably the dog-faced fruit bat, fluttered past on its way to some fruit trees found growing in the compound of the inn. On a corner of the ceiling above my head, an atlas moth, the largest moth in the world, seemed desperate to move on. Exhausted, I called it a day.

The next morning, we had another boat trip but a little further towards the middle of the lake. The research scientists were busy taking water samples to be brought back for analysis in the labs on campus. It has been routine tasks for them to keep monitoring the water quality of Tasik Chini and document both the terrestrial and aquatic biodiversity encountered within this UNESCO biosphere reserve. I caught sight of numerous slender pale-green pitchers of *Nepenthes gracilis* hanging against the backdrop of lush *Pandanus* stands. The slow passage through the narrow water channels allowed me to observe closely at the aquatic plant species growing just submersed or above the lake surface. Tasik Chini is richly endowed with unique wetland habitat that supports a variety of beautiful aquatic plants, such as the submersed cat's tail, *Cabomba furcata,* which blooms purple, giving the lake its postcard-quality vista I had previously seen featured in *Going Places,* the in-flight magazine of our national carrier, the Malaysian Airlines.

My eyes were again absolutely fixated to the stunning beauty of the lotus blooms. The radiance of pink hues emanating from them were simply intoxicating. I was appalled to learn that all this brilliance and beauty was narrowly obliterated a few years back. Its pristine status was almost wiped out through man's short-sightedness, ignorance, and greed. As far back as the 1970s, Tasik Chini has been adversely affected by the human activities around it. Deforestations, logging, mining, and palm oil plantations resulted in huge loads of sediments eroding and settling in the lakes, rivers, and tributaries. For years, the lake seemed to cope well through seasonal flushing of the sediments and other organic debris in the water body. Then, in 1994, came a decision to build a damn in Sungai Chini, a narrow tributary that connects Sungai Pahang to the lake. For all its intents and purposes, the construction of a dam was a noble one. Tasik Chini was then a rising star as a tourist destination, all set to bring huge tourism revenue for the state of Pahang. There was, however, a small problem. In the dry season, the water at a few places along Sungai Chini was too shallow to ply tourist boats. Tourists had to alight at several locations whilst their boats were dragged to deeper parts and continue their trip to the lake. Building a dam to maintain a higher water level along Sungai Chini seemed like a clear-cut solution. It would avoid the need for tourists to get off the boat and get their feet wet, so they thought. Unfortunately, the construction of the dam turned out to be a poorly conceived idea. It resulted in an ecological disaster. Soon after the dam construction was completed, Tasik Chini showed dramatic changes in its hydrological regime. Its overall water level significantly rose, causing many unpredicted adverse consequences. Huge tracts of both lakeside and riverine habitats were inundated and rendered unproductive. Widespread soil erosions occurred at record-breaking pace, exposing massive networks of roots that have remained concealed in the riverbanks for eons. Majestic trees that used to line the riverbanks, streams, and lakesides succumbed and fell unaided. The river and lake water bodies were filled with dead remains of once vibrant and lush greeneries. Water oxygenation levels fell, resulting in eutrophication and algal blooms. Signs of lake eutrophication began to show when green and blue algae flourished in the lake. Along with it, much of Lake Chini's biological functions were compromised. Its associated flora and fauna suffered.

The rise in the water level had significant effects on the biodiversity of the lake and surrounding areas. Populations of riverine species of plants and unique aquatic plant species growing in the lake were reported to have declined as a result of drowning. Within the lake, the principal breeding sites for many species of fish were lost. Populations of some endemic fish species have also declined. Tasik Chini was previously used by many species of migratory birds. It is a matter of speculation that the number of birds and bird species using the lake watershed may have also declined. The populations and diversity of mammal and reptile species in the area too may have been affected adversely. Today, only small scattered patches of primary rainforests remain around the lake.

The poor decision to construct the damn was realised in the nick of time before an ecological disaster struck beyond repair. After a thorough assessment of the damage and adverse consequences associated with that ill-conceived idea, a team of researchers from UKM applied for Tasik Chini to be accorded the status of UNESCO biosphere reserve. This would facilitate more systematic scientific studies to be undertaken aimed at generating data needed to bring back the lake to its near-pristine state prior to the dam construction. My visit to Tasik Chini left me with an impression that such thinking would not be a pie in the sky. Active ecological research has started to yield useful data already.

Indeed, Malaysia's first UNESCO designated biosphere reserve is an area of unique biodiversity worthy of protection and preservation. The isolation and expanse of this freshwater catchment area makes this place an island of biodiversity. It is an out-of-the-ordinary ecosystem where species have evolved and adapted to strive successfully, spawning unique flora and fauna found nowhere else in the world. A safe haven for over two hundred species of tropical birds, Tasik Chini ebbs and fluctuates in size with the seasonal monsoons. It can continue to become a popular destination for ecotourism and generate revenue for the state government. In November to January, the lake swells to create a fishing haven for anglers; whilst during October to March, this tranquil freshwater sanctuary becomes a transit for migratory birds from the northern parts of Asia. Protection of this important area will ensure they have a place to seek reprieve from the punishing cold winter. The biosphere reserve provides food, shelter, and water for these migratory birds to continue on their long journey south. Against the orange sky of a setting sun, the sight of hundreds of migratory birds mingling with resident birds reinforces this crucial need to rejuvenate Tasik Chini to its original natural state. As countries throughout the planet strive to become economic behemoths at the expense of the environment, our biosphere reserves like Tasik Chini could one day be the primary reason to visit Malaysia. Tasik Chini is truly a Mother Nature's gem to be treasured. To lose it would be to lose an invaluable treasure for future generations.

A NOSE JOB GONE WRONG?

MY ELDEST DAUGHTER, AZIZAH, WAS in Sabah for a family holiday. Her husband, Stephen, has always been enthusiastic about nature. Their children, Nate and Caspar, too, need to be encouraged to love nature and respect the environment. After an evening of deliberations on where to go during their week's stay, we agreed on making a day trip to Weston, a small town two-hour drive out of Kota Kinabalu. This is a popular destination for viewing the proboscis monkeys and fireflies. Nate had seen proboscis monkeys on TV and in books, but he would love to see this funny-looking creature in the wild. That would be an awesome Borneo experience. Our wildlife sighting adventure includes a boat ride to the mangrove forests where these monkeys are found. We hope Caspar, hardly a year old then, would be able to stand the boat ride.

The crisp morning air was so refreshing, blowing across our faces as our boatman sped along the river towards the mangroves about two-kilometre distance from the jetty. On arrival, he turned off the outboard engines and allowed the boat to slowly drift towards the riverbank. Everyone was silent in full anticipation of what's next. Instantaneously, I felt the reigning peace and tranquillity I had been craving for. I dug up the camera from my backpack to be duly prepared for some great shots. No wildlife, monkeys, or birds in sight yet. I killed time gunning my zoom lenses along the edges of the riverbanks, manually focusing up and down the lush foliage of some riverine plants. Discernable through the view finder were numerous small pinkish and purplish flowers against the green monotonous landscapes of the mangroves. The surface of the river was still with the boat engine now turned off. No one was speaking, but their eyes were busy scanning the landscape to detect any movement up the trees. Everyone on board seemed anxiously anticipating what would be spotted amidst the peaceful surrounds.

I looked out over the reflecting swamp as the hot morning sun beamed its rays on the wild creatures still deep in their slumber. Life around us began to stir. Birds started their day flying and calling; true to the axiom 'The early bird catches the worms.' I could feel the back of my neck being caressed by the soft touches of the morning breeze. Quietly we sat, and patiently we waited for any signs of life yonder. Caspar had quietly fallen asleep being lullabied by the sounds and freshness of nature around him. Suddenly, a ruckus hit! A chaotic scene of crashing noises and wild commotions amongst the branches and leaves above. A couple of furry brown creatures had just made a huge ominous leap from a tree of considerable height down. It was a clumsy performance, but they seemed to have landed safely on branches a few metres away from where our boat was. Startled, everyone almost jumped out of their skin. That jolted us to attention. A pair of proboscis monkeys was staring down at us. A pastel-coloured infant, not more than a few weeks old, was precariously clinging to the mother's fur. They were just as surprised to see us. 'Greetings, a pleasure meeting you guys!' I heard myself whispering under my breath to calm my heart beating fast with excitement. 'How cute and caring.' I heaved a sigh as I reached for my camera. Glaring from its grey-pinkish face, the infant's huge gleaming eyes were fixated on me as I cautiously raised the oversized zoom lens hanging from my neck. I tried to frame in a group photo of the entire family. The infant's head was awkwardly positioned upside down, sticking out from the mother's brown coating below her chin. My mind flashed back to a magazine photograph I once saw of the late superstar Michael Jackson dangling his baby out of a window from his New York apartment. That created an uproar criticising Michael for putting his baby in danger of accidental slip from his arms.

But Michael wasn't a monkey! Both the mother and baby proboscis seemed cool and absolutely sanguine. I managed to get a few great family shots nonetheless.

Infants of proboscis monkeys are born with their faces vivid blue in colour. At the age of two months, their facial colour darkens to sooty dark grey but lightens to the flesh colour of the adult at around eight months. They would stay in close proximity to their mother for about one year till they have acquired much of the living skills to survive on their own. This prolonged stay with the family not only protects them from potential predators but also imbues them with social roles they must play when they finally leave the troop.

The pendulous nose of a male Proboscis entitles him to have many wives living in a harem with his many offspring. But as he gets on in life and feels his age, he will be displaced by a younger and more virile male to reign over his harem.

I heard another commotion originating from amongst the adjacent forests, this time boisterously and raucously. Some adult monkeys were bouncing and jumping rowdily. At the same time, they were letting out forceful vocal sounds and displaying facial expressions at each other. Proboscis monkeys, like macaques, employ both sounds and looks to convey their intentions to rival males and potential mates. A yawn, for instance, should not to be taken as just a typical meaningless gesture or sign of exhaustion. Yawning of one male to another could be a fully alert threat display. Staring could also be a threat. In response to a yawn, other males would look down or away to avoid direct confrontations. Fierce fighting are prevented most of the times. I couldn't help feeling slightly intimidated when a large male proboscis turned to face me displaying a series of threatening facial expressions. Without a doubt, he was communicating with me. He was warning me from approaching any further, essentially saying, 'Stay out, this is our territory.' I offered no argument and respectfully heeded by staying put. I was more than happy to just stand and observe from afar.

Found only in Borneo, proboscis monkeys are specialised denizens of the mangrove forests. The monkey's body is mostly covered with ginger-orange short furs except for the areas around the pot belly and along the lower limbs and its unusually long tail. The Indonesians were the first to call this ugly, or beautiful whichever you fancy, animal *monyet belanda*, literally translated as 'Dutchman monkey'. The locals must have felt the monkeys resembled the Dutch traders in their exceptionally hairy body, red face, big nose, and bulging pot belly—familiar features of a Dutchman sailor who had just landed from sea travel during the colonial times.

Of all primates, proboscis monkeys have the longest nose, often as long as seven inches, which is roughly a quarter of their body length. Its long nose, hanging like a pendulum of the grandfather clock in my living room, is enough to get its scientific name, *Nasalis larvatus*; nasalis being the name of the small muscle on each side of the nose capable of constricting and making the nose flare with a pair of gaping nostrils. It is almost comical to watch them plucking and shoving leaves into the mouth that is constantly obstructed by the pendulous nose. I wonder why bother to have a nose that awkwardly hangs over the mouth only to get in the way during feeding? I pointed this out to my two grandsons and asked them to watch how candidly the animal would push his nose up and out of the way when he was enjoying his feast of the mangrove leaves. And when he looked up to select another handful of leaves, the nose would flop back up and smack him between the eyes. A clumsy and sloppy eater. It was perhaps nature's design to give female proboscis a more 'ladylike' disposition by giving them a dainty pointed nose instead.

Unlike the males, female Proboscis monkeys have dainty tilted up nose. Perhaps having a ridiculously huge nose would be unsightly and unappealing for attracting mating partners.

Nate was all quiet standing next to me looking very deeply in thoughts. I could somehow guess what was playing in his little mind. I had explained to him a while back that an elephant trunk isn't quite a real nose but essentially an extended nose fused with the elephant's top lip. The fused lip functions as opposable 'fingers' enabling the elephant to grasp small objects with the trunk. It comes handy like we use our thumbs to grab stuff. He must be wondering whether what he was seeing on the proboscis monkey now is a trunk or a real nose. Nate was smitten to be looking at the longest real nose he had ever seen. He looked up at me and asked, 'Grandpa, but why would he have such a long nose when he has real fingers to grab stuff with?'

That was a good question, but I knew the answer to that would be quite lengthy as well. So as not to distract ourselves from observing more bizarre antics of the proboscis monkeys in front of us, I decided to postpone answering Nate's question in scientific terms but sufficed to quip, 'That's because he has been telling a lot of lies. You know what happens to Pinocchio's nose every time he tells a lie, don't you?'

Nate put on a smirked face and shook his head. 'Ahhh . . . Grandpa.'

Female Proboscis keeps a close watch on her offspring bouncing about like our toddlers jumping and scampering on beds and couches. For Proboscis juveniles, this monkeying around are performed way up high on trees and branches at the risk of accidentally falling to the ground and break their bones or into the water where crocodiles might be waiting.

If you ask me, 'What's the most bizarre-looking animal in Borneo?' I would unhesitatingly say, 'The proboscis monkey.' Indeed, beauty is in the eyes of the beholder. I recalled a field trip taking my students to see proboscis monkeys in Klias Peninsula, Sabah, when I was the dean of science at UKM Sabah in the mid-1980s. I was explaining to my students that the alpha male of the proboscis monkey lives in a harem of up to fifteen females. The female proboscis seems to be attracted to the male with larger and longer nose. One of the female students then asked, 'Why would the females get attracted to the ugliest male? I would have thought a male with proportionately sized nose and flat non-bulging stomach would be the hot one. Not a sloppy fat slob.'

65

But such colossal and disproportionate nose is more than meets the eye to the amorous female proboscis. His sex appeal is an asset of choice. Somehow, females are attracted to the big-nosed males. In the world of the proboscis monkeys, nose size matters. The bigger the better, it seems. This is evident from the bigger number of females kept in the harem of big-nosed males. Small-nosed males have smaller number of females in their harems. Furthermore, the older male individuals into their sunset years of reproductive life seem to have smaller nose. Perhaps they no longer find the need to have sex appeal.

This bizarre behaviour where oversized nose drive female proboscis wildly sexy has received genetic investigations. If males possessing huge noses are preferred for mating, it would be advantageous if this trait be inherited from one generation to another. It has been shown the genes determining this long-nose trait are indeed passed on to the next generations. Hence, the 'status symbol' genes are specifically selected and preserved within the species. Blessed would be the individuals endowed with humongous nose with respect to their sexual activities. Proboscis monkeys live in a harem comprising one dominant male and around six sexually matured females. Group size varies with some making up to as high as thirty individuals including their offspring. The ruling 'king' will be kept busy in procreating healthy 'subjects' of future harems. Hence, robust genes inherited within their populations would be important to ensure the survival and continuance of the species.

There have been other theories on why male proboscis monkeys are endowed with such exceptionally long nose. These monkeys are known to be proficient swimmers. It is suggested that the nose could function as a snorkel when swimming by somehow placing it above water for breathing. But female proboscis swim just as well without a pendulous nose. So that theory doesn't seem to hold water. Another suggestion alluding to the possible function of such oversized nose is for cooling the animal. The nose could help to radiate excess body heat more efficiently. The massive size could conceivably increase the surface area of the nose lined with small blood vessels. On a hot day, these blood vessels are capable of dilating to allow for heat loss more efficient, keeping the animal cool. This ability to maximise heat loss would cool the monkeys from the sweltering heat of the sun. He would find this especially welcoming and beneficial whilst sitting high on the trees directly in the sun feeding on the young leaves found in abundance at the top of the mangroves.

Long Is Sexy

The male proboscis monkey wouldn't trade his long nose for the world. That ridiculously ugly nose comes with almost an entitlement to a polygamous relationship with several females. A dominant male has been seen living in a harem with as many as seven concubines at a time. Big noses feature predominantly in the sex life of proboscis monkeys. A big nose is a sexual asset that meets the approval of female partners. Males with bigger nose have more females in their harem than those with smaller nose. Size does matter after all.

Despite such huge and long noses, the proboscis monkeys don't have super-smelling power. Their sense of smell is no better than other monkeys with much smaller noses. But this nose story doesn't end just yet. The male nose also has another function. It acts like a loudspeaker or a hailer. The ability to make himself heard louder would be most useful in marshalling his females and youngsters in his troop. The males with louder vocalisations are able to communicate with females in distant locations through honking. Any looming threats or danger to members of his harem, the nose would become enlarged, allowing blood to rush in filling the nasal tissue. The swollen nose then would be transformed into a resonating chamber capable of amplifying the honking sound. Louder honks would sound more threatening to other hostile males in the proximity or become more audible for attracting potential mating partners.

There are various kinds of calls. Proboscis are known to produce specific honks for different purposes. A growl is made by adult male to calm down another member in the group. A honk is an aggressive call meant as a threat to members of other groups. On hearing this, other males would be intimidated with the loud harsh voices of the dominant male and tend to stay away from the harem. They also honk in the presence of predators. Loud honking noises warn the young offspring about the presence of nearby predators such as pythons, clouded leopards, and crocodiles. Soft honks are used to pacify and assure infants of their safety and comfort. Harsher honks would warn them of danger. Juveniles of both sexes and adult females do not honk but emit a piercing shriek when they become agitated or excited. A scream is also heard during agonistic or combative interactions, usually heard during feeding bouts and at night before sleep. With such over-arching roles of their noses, there is no question about the need for proboscis monkeys going for a nose job, is there?

Besides honking, proboscis also display body movements to communicate. To keep other males off his females, the dominant male would make loud spectacular leaping displays but rarely result in actual contact. Social grooming is also used to reinforce the bonds between individuals. Unlike the macaques, grooming in proboscis seems like a brief interlude, usually lasting not more than five minutes. Performed with both individuals in a sitting posture, the groomer would use the hands or the teeth to pick stuff found in their furs.

A baby of Proboscis is born with vivid blue face and constantly kept clean through grooming. Parental investment is high with the mother providing her baby milk and nursing till about 7 months old before switching to diets consisting of young shoots and foliage.

As I was silently marvelling at the antics of proboscis and its many adaptations to living in the mangroves, I was at the mercy of pesky mosquitoes. I put myself to be constantly persecuted by clouds of mangrove mosquitoes hovering over my head, my neck, and my arms. Whilst male mosquitoes are content to live of the nectar and juices from plants, the females aren't. They get their nourishment from the blood of people or animals. First-time visitors to the mangroves often suffer unusual itching and swelling after being bitten by these blood-sucking pests. My thoughts drifted to a friend, Prof Ramesh Boonratana, a.k.a. Zimbo, of Mahidol University, Thailand. Researching for his doctoral thesis in the 1980s, Zimbo carried out years of field trips observing groups of proboscis monkeys in this same stretch on mangrove forests. Now, I truly admire his guts and dedication to be working under these horrific conditions. He must have a magic portion to avoid becoming a meal to these vicious blood-sucking creatures.

In their natural habitats, proboscis monkeys live in groups exclusively in riverine forests, mangroves, and peat swamps. A group size ranges from thirteen to thirty-two individuals. Not a territorial species, one group might overlap with other groups with respect to feeding or breeding ranges. Because they are highly dependent on habitats that adjoin rivers, they are never seen farther than 600 metres from a river or stream. Most active from late afternoon to dark, they might move away to the nipah forest in the morning and back into the mangroves in the afternoon.

Living in the wild affords a better chance in succeeding if animals were to function as a group. Living alone without the help of others could leave one to many risks. Unsuspecting predators could be lurking from nowhere amidst the lush green backdrops of the mangroves. Group living also helps in finding food. It would be easier with more pairs of eyes helping to locate the food sources. Animals can also come together to hunt for prey. Proboscis monkeys are amongst the many types of primates known to unite in the wild. It has become a natural phenomenon to warn each other, especially the young, of impending danger or availability of food.

In addition to baring teeth, opening mouths, leaping and shaking branches, male Proboscis communicate using different vocalizations. Special honks are used when talking to females, infants or other males and warning them of danger. After doing his job and feasting on a hearty meal of the tannin-rich mangrove leaves, a male proboscis can be seen dozing off in recluse high up on a branch.

Proboscis monkeys not only live in groups but also have a well-defined social structure. They live in two types of groups: the bachelor group and the one-male harem. Bachelor groups consist of around five to ten male monkeys with no dominant leaders. The harem consists of one dominant male and about fifteen females. The male will be the 'head of the family', becoming a master of all females and their babies. But females can be promiscuous. They can freely change membership amongst the harems. Adult females will sometimes leave their one-male group and join another one-male group. But the adult male will not tolerate the presence of another male in his harem. So the maturing males in the party must be cautious as they approach the age at which his presence might be considered a threat to the status of the presiding male. Young males are kicked out of the one-male group once they reach adolescence at about eighteen months of age. He would then join a bachelor group to still benefit from group living.

Groups will come together during the evening near rivers to sleep in trees. They will also meet and travel together during the day. Their social structure appears to have distinct gender roles. In the one-male harem group, the adult female tends to coordinate and lead the group when moving. It is the duty of the male to ensure the individuals of his group, scattered feeding out in the open, are free of any danger. He would post sentinels around the feeding ground to keep a look out for predators. He will only intervene during the movement and feeding when female-female agonistic interactions happen. The dominant male has also been seen to interfere and protect juveniles from female aggression. Females in the harem do compete with each other to get the attention of the only male and copulate. It is understandable that grooming, which serves to forge bonding amongst members of the harem, is done only by females.

The role of the male in procreating and ensuring robust formation of future harems is important. Whilst heading the group, the dominant male would try to father healthy offspring, which is biologically crucial for the continuance of the species. He seems to be continually preoccupied with sex. He would want to mate and produce his own offspring as many and as quickly as possible. He knows he has to pass on his 'big nose' genes before his time is up. The time will soon come when he will be displaced by younger mature males from the bachelor groups. When this happens, he will be banished from his harem, and all dependent infants in the harem will be killed by the victorious male. This is done by the new dominant male to get the female monkeys pregnant with his own offspring as quickly as possible.

Proboscis monkeys are highly arboreal, jumping from tree to tree. Only very rarely would they come to the ground or riverbanks to drink. They live primarily on leaves, which make up 95 per cent of their diet. Because leaves are so poor in nutrients, a proboscis has to eat a lot of leaves. Hence, it has to spend most of its time looking for food and eating them until its stomach contents can make up one-quarter of its body weight. An adult can munch up to 1,800 of the bitter tannic mangrove leaves. Like cows and other leaf eaters, it has a large stomach divided into compartments equipped with fermentation chambers where digestion is facilitated by special cellulose-digesting bacteria. Proboscis stomach is twice as large as other colobines with similar digestive system. This gives them a permanently pregnant look, even the males. They rarely need to drink, getting all their water from the leaves. They gather food and feed together before roosting on neighbouring trees for the night. Despite their large size of up to twenty kilograms, proboscis monkeys are not territorial. They will tolerate other groups in their feeding areas. In this respect, they are often considered one of the most docile species of primates. Sometimes they are too accommodating that macaques and orangutans have been seen to displace proboscis monkey at feeding sites.

Nerves of Steel

In equestrian, training a horse to jump is a professional job requiring a lot of patience and dedication. It takes time for the horse to be comfortable with small jumps and incrementally advance to competitive heights. Immense amount of hours is required in training, exercising, and working the nerves of prized horses before they can gain enough confidence to make huge jumps. But for the proboscis monkeys, making big jumps seem to be intrinsically gifted. They have been seen making phenomenal jumps across huge gaps from treetops to another. It's in their nature to do this in search of young juicy mangrove leaves to eat. In groups, they are often sighted leaping across crocodile-infested rivers. Landing in the waters, they would hurriedly swim up the opposite bank, escaping the lurking predators. Interestingly, it's a female that frequently takes the lead in this leap of faith. In these creatures, courage and confidence seem inborn. They all seem to have the nerves of steel.

Proboscis monkeys often leap directly into the water in an attempt to get to new food sources across the river. But the sound from their splash can spell danger. Marauding crocodiles would hear the splash from up to 200 meters away and swim towards it with the hope members of the more monkeys follow suit and dive; giving an opportunity for a hearty meal.

Proboscis monkeys often leap directly into the water in an attempt to get to new food sources across the river. But the sound from their splash can spell danger. Marauding crocodiles would hear the splash from up to 200 meters away and swim towards it with the hope members of the more monkeys follow suit and dive; giving an opportunity for a hearty meal.

Proboscis monkeys are accomplished swimmers. Some consider them the best primate swimmer. But they swim only when necessary, not for pleasure. They can swim underwater for up to twenty metres if disturbed suddenly. Their interdigital webbing is an adaptation for swimming. With their partially webbed back feet, they are able to do the dog paddle, which they use to slip quietly into the water and move silently in water without splashing. In search of food or escaping from predators, they would walk or swim across river. They have adopted several interesting river-crossing behaviours to avoid predators found in the rivers, especially the false gavial and crocodiles. Before crossing, they would scan visually across the water surfaces for any lurking predator. Then strategically they would choose the narrowest points across the rivers and move cautiously in a single file line. The males tend to be the last individuals to cross amongst group members. In the presence of other groups, they would unite to cross rivers in large numbers, keeping watch on each other and totally weary of the presence of lurking crocodiles. Sometimes they would use foliage to 'springboard' across rivers. They would enter the water and swim quietly, but as soon as they cross over, they would exit in a huge leap onto the bank and hurry up a tree. These sensible and coordinated crossings of rivers as a troop could be an anti-predator behaviour that this species has learned over the years.

The pink purplish penis of male Proboscis is constantly erect in full view of the females at all times. Such penile erection called tumescence is common in mammals but its function in Proboscis is anyone's guess.

I cast my last inspection of the silent troop's feeding, half scrutinising and half admiring the awesome works of Mother Nature. I jealously thought of the privileged males of each group. I found myself smiling noticing the penis protruding from the black-coloured scrotum. His genitalia is perennially erect. It sticks up like a red hot chili between his outspread legs. Its strikingly maroon-red penis could be serving to attract notice and attention of amorous females from a distance. I have not come across any scientific explanation as to why and how this permanent tumescence occurs. In humans, tumescence is the normal flow of blood into the blood vessels of the penis, causing it to harden and become erect. This usually signals sexual excitation and possible readiness for sexual activity. Primatologists have not figured out whether tumescence in the proboscis monkeys could also be an aspect of sexual display. I tried to look for any clues if the males were preoccupied with sex at all. They seemed to sit with their legs akimbo, fully displaying their perennially erect genitals. Females, in contrast, sat with their legs closed, prim and proper like ladies. Studies have shown that a majority of copulations in this species are initiated by females, indicating that it is the females that chose the male to mate with. She would signal her choice by displaying in front of him. She would start by making a pout face, pursing the lips followed by head shaking. This seems to be the behaviour pattern performed by the female telling the male she is ready for copulation. The male would mount from the rear, grabbing the partner at the midsection with the hands and her rear legs with the feet. Most copulatory bouts consist of single thrusts. During mating, juveniles would often harass the male whilst he is mounting the female. Living in a harem as the male is accustomed to, this could be the answer to why the penis was strikingly red and perennially erect. Shaking my head, smiling, I sighed. 'No such thing as ED or erectile dysfunction amongst this species of primates for sure!' I resigned with the thought that Viagra would not be a hot item amongst these guys!

Infanticide, the act of killing babies within the species, does occur in the primate world, especially during competition for food or sexual selection. The role of the male Proboscis in parental care is primarily providing protection for his vulnerable offspring by excluding potentially infanticidal rival males from the group.

By late afternoon, the almost saturated humid air was making everyone uncomfortable. Spending the last hour on a stationary boat didn't help. The ferocious mosquitoes had sensed our presence, and soon everyone was agonising over bites from these savage blood suckers. It was time to take a breather and have something to bite at one of the eateries in Weston.

As darkness crept in, the mangroves and riverbanks lighted up with tiny glittering yellows. Our boatman asked if Nathaniel and Caspar were all ready for their next adventure. The next plan was to slowly cruise along the river to see nature's most magnificent light display. I caught sight of small yellow lights flickering at a distance only to float away into the darkness. They are congregating fireflies known as *kunang-kunang* in Malay, soft-bodied beetles not exceeding twenty-five millimetres in length. On the underside of their abdomen, these diminutive insects are equipped with special light organs capable of glowing in luminous flashes. There are over 2,000 firefly species in the world. But the congregating firefly of Sabah is the most impressive. They belong to the genus *Pteroptyx* and have the habit of gathering and flashing in numbers ranging from hundreds to thousands of individuals per group. The aspect that makes them so enchanting is their ability to create one of the most delightful displays of lights, giving that unmistakable Christmas atmosphere. Nathaniel and Caspar must be thinking Christmas comes earlier in Weston than London. The panoramic view of flashing lights coming from silhouettes of drooping tropical trees conjured images of mystic, mysterious, intriguing, or even haunting. This wonderful natural phenomenon has been fascinating humans since time immemorial.

But, alas, they are not there to feast our human eyes. These flickers of light are but a means of communication—a sort of insect Morse code. Female fireflies would repeatedly emit lights in a specific frequency pattern that acts as a signal to attract males of their species closer. The light signals serve to bring both sexes together for mating to occur. Hence, the courtship is brief and relies on each other's ability to recognise the pulses of light signals characteristic of their own species. Indeed, the firefly love story has a straightforward plot.

But not all love affairs in the firefly world have a happy ending. Using flashing lights to attract mating partners can prove fatal in some genus of fireflies. Females of the firefly *Photuris* found in South America have been shown to be sneaky, deceitful crooks. They have an appetite for other fireflies, making a meal of male firefly from a different genus, *Photinus*. *Photuris* fireflies have an ingenious strategy to get their food. The females have learned to produce flashing patterns of *Photinus* species. The hungry female *Photuris* would mimic a female of *Photinus* species with fake flashes. Seeing and recognising these fake flashes as from their own females, the *Photinus* males would fly closer until it is too late. They are tricked into fatality. Instead of finding a mate, they end up as meals for females from another genus. It is not clear if such risky love affair also occurs in the *Pteroptyx* genus of Sabah fireflies.

Fireflies produce flashing to identify members of the opposite sex and attract them for mating.

The sheer spectacle of how a mangrove ecosystem established itself has always fascinated me. The persistence and dynamics of its formation is phenomenal. The ebbing tide slowly but surely nibbled away at the land. The blackish sandy banks bordering the mangroves gradually eroded away, discharging tons of silt and mud into the sea. This created habitats favourable for the growth and establishment of specialised plant communities. Salt-tolerant mangrove species grow well here on the newly formed soft muddy substratum. Specialised animals evolve and adapt to thrive in this unique tropical ecosystem.

My mind is suddenly grappling with the questions pertaining to the future of the proboscis monkeys within these mangroves. Within the last four decades, the population of proboscis monkeys has dwindled by 80 per cent. Their low reproductive nature adds to the population problem. The proboscis monkey gives birth to a single offspring. The gestation length for this species is about 170 days. With the exception of orangutan, this rate of reproduction is considered low amongst other primates. During child delivery, the female would sit on her side amongst the foliage of several hardy branches and give birth. This typically lasts not more than five minutes. It has been reported the mother would candidly eat the placenta after delivery has taken place. The scientific basis for this bizarre behaviour remains speculative.

Proboscis has low reproductive rate giving birth to a single offspring after a gestation of 166 days. Low birth rate and having a lifespan of not more than 23 years place them high on the endangered list of species heading for extinction.

Habitat destruction and hunting remain the two greatest threats to these adorable creatures. Their primary habitats, the mangroves, have been cleared extensively for economic development including aquaculture and human settlements. In some parts of Borneo, proboscis monkeys are hunted for food. Their somewhat unhurried and graceful nature in the wild makes them easy targets. Sabah has seen rapid economic progress in recent decades. Adversely, the mangroves have been under severe threat from human settlements, logging, and land clearing for aquaculture and plantations. Urbanisation and increasing demand for mangrove products, such as materials for buildings and fuel, have led to the destruction and degradation of mangrove forests throughout Borneo. Since proboscis monkeys only thrive on young leaves, fruits, and seeds of certain species of riverine and mangrove vegetations, they are forced to travel and find enough food. This means the species needs large protected areas to continue surviving. Because of this, proboscis monkeys have been recently classified a strictly protected species. One comforting news is they are no longer hunted as much as the orangutans. They do poorly in captivity and need a huge supply of mangrove leaves to survive. In this respect, they are not sought after as pets unlike their cousins, the white-handed gibbons and orangutan babies. Definitely a blessing in disguise for the proboscis.

One fine night, the full term pregnant female sits on a branch within the foliage to give birth to a baby with purplish-blue coloured face. The mother almost immediately consumes the placenta; a peculiar behaviour that still defy a scientific explanation.

If I were tasked with choosing just one ecosystem to safeguard the future of humankind on this planet, mangroves would be my strong contender.

This is because climate change, in my view, would be the next biggest challenge for our survival as a species. Those mucky, tangled coastal mangroves serve us to absorb and blunt storm surges during catastrophic weather havocs. They protect us from devastating tsunamis. They act as nurseries where a stunning array of marine species are nurtured before going out to mature at sea. They guarantee us with sufficient supply of seafood. But there is more. Not many of us appreciate the fact that mangroves also store vast amounts of carbon. Mangrove forest is one of the most productive forest ecosystems in terms of its efficiency to store carbon. It is able to stockpile carbon per unit area three times more than other tropical forests. The role of mangrove forests in carbon sequestering and subverting global warming is immense. Acre per acre, mangroves 'are the world champions of carbon sequestration', said Neil Saintilan, an ecologist at Macquarie University in Sydney.

We arrived back at the jetty in good time. Stephen, Azizah, Nate, and Caspar were all quiet and looking washed out. The day's outing must have zapped out all the energy in them. As we walked to the car park, I scanned the edges of the water that seemed to be ebbing. The air was still crisp and fresh. I knew I would be craving for the reigning tranquillity as soon as we got back to my condominium in the city. Tired, the children placed their heads against the car windows and dozed off. I turned off my camera after reviewing all the shots taken for the day. My brain was delirious, and my mind wouldn't sleep like my grandchildren. The many chanced encounters of the day consumed my thoughts. There was no simple description to the aura of satisfaction and the unending anxiety about what we have seen and experienced today. An awesome experience and what a feeling! Granted we weren't anywhere near to *Star Trek*'s mission of 'to boldly go where no man has gone before', but we were close enough. Memorable moments indeed.

ELTON JOHN'S
RAINFOREST PROTÉGÉ

WAY BACK IN 1969 AT the University of Otago, New Zealand, I found myself in a quandary—caught between a rock and a hard place. I was forced to come to a decision on what area of specialisation I would like to pursue for my undergraduate studies. It was a toss between two disciplines: geology versus biology. I couldn't quite picture myself getting all keyed up finding out how the Earth's surface behaved or what rocks were made of. But I would be inclined to spend the next three years at the university learning how living things came to being, work, and function. That would stir my curiosity more than lifeless rocks and fossils, I figured then. In essence, it came to this: 'Which of the two I fancied more, the theory of plate tectonics or the theory of evolution?' Decidedly, I opted for biology. That was the beginning of my career as a biological scientist with a leaning towards health science and immunology. So when I heard about Langkawi being designated as Malaysia's first geopark, I was naturally curious to know what I have been missing out on. How could rocks of Langkawi be accorded such global mark of distinction?

Coincidentally, I was playing host to an old acquaintance, Stanly, a geology professor from the United States. I met Stan during my

83

sabbatical leave at the University of Michigan, Ann Arbor, in 1985. He came to present his research on oceanography and fossil records at an International Geological Congress held in Kuala Lumpur. Fuelled by my newfound curiosity about rocks and stuff related to geology, I suggested we fly to Pulau Langkawi for a few days after his conference to which he unhesitatingly agreed. I looked forward to an educational excursion with my foreign guest; pretty certain of gaining some interesting insights on the geological history of this geopark island from him.

Like turquoise gemstones randomly scattered across the deep blue ocean below, we caught sight of Langkawi Island. From the air, we gasped at the sight of white sandy beaches and vast open seas. Essentially a diminutive archipelago, this island paradise lies some thirty kilometres off the mainland of north-western Peninsular Malaysia. The chain of islands stretches out into the deep blue expanse of the Andaman Sea as a cluster of ninety-nine islands, plus another four during low tide.

Lugging our bags to the car rental counter, we were impressed with the moderately busy modern airport. The short drive by road to our resort hotel took us through a series of panoramic backdrops of turquoise seas, lime-green paddy fields, and luscious forest-clad distant hills. We were rightly awestruck with what greeted us. It was easy to fall in love with Langkawi.

Life seemed unhurried here. It gave you that cavalier and laid-back ambience starkly differing from that of the mainland. The hotel we were staying consisted of rows of above-water chalets jutting out to sea. Facing the vast open sea, a hammock hung and swayed invitingly on each porch of the rooms. All over we were met with friendly faces brimming with smiles and gracious casual chats. Donning a contagious affable twinkle myself, I sensed that we could end up staying here for longer than we planned.

The next day, Stan and I were up early before the morning got too hot. One would never have guessed that the cool and peaceful ambience of your air-conditioned hotel rooms was in effect surrounded by hot and humid virgin rainforests. The lush tropical rainforest played home for a host of fascinating faunal species, a rich diversity of tropical birds, insects, and other rainforest animals. A bizarre, beguiling blend of wildlife and modern hotels would be one of Langkawi's best-kept secrets. Here, it wasn't uncommon for tourists staying at posh five-star hotels to step out of their rooms and come face to face with rare tropical animals not easily encountered on the peninsular mainland.

Stan and I decided to get closer to the songs of birds and shrills of crickets coming from the patch of forests fringing our chalet. Earlier that morning, peering out of the window, I caught a glimpse of fleeting furry black figures dashing in and out amongst the branches and green foliage at a distance. The accompanying screeching calls seemed to be getting closer. It was a group of spectacled monkeys or dusky leaf monkeys, *Trachypithecus obscurus*. Acrobatically swinging from tree to tree, they were foraging on succulent young leaves and shoots of a ficus tree just a few metres away from the path leading to our chalet. Oblivious to our intrusion and cameras clicking away, a few adult individuals descended to the ground to feed on low shrubs. Stan had never seen such creatures before. He was absolutely thrilled to see the thick white eye rings and pale-pinkish skin around the mouth, devoid of fur.

'Look at those adorable little faces. Those white spectacles on them were so comical yet so endearing!' he exclaimed.

'Yes, they happen to be the biggest fan of the rock star Sir Elton John,' I quipped.

The distinctive feature of the dusky leaf monkey is its circular rings around the eyes, which give an appearance of a spectacle. Hence, dusky leaf monkey is also known as spectacled leaf monkey.

I enlightened Stan on the distribution of spectacled leaf monkeys in this part of the world. They are found majorly on Malay Peninsula, Thailand, and Southern Burma. A few locations in Peninsular Malaysia are particularly known to harbour big friendly communities of these adorable monkeys, including the islands of Penang, Langkawi, and Perhentian Besar. They are also a source of endearment in public parks and botanical gardens such as those inhabiting patches of forests in Lake Garden, Taiping, and Botanical Garden, Penang.

Another characteristic feature of dusky leaf monkey is its buffy crown and creamy patch over the mouth. They are similar to other langurs in their anatomy and thereby do not have many unique adaptations in their diet and foraging behaviour. The body length of a dusky leaf monkey is usually around forty to sixty centimetres and weighs between five and nine kilograms. An amazing fact is that with such light weight and small size, it can consume two kilograms of food per day.

Stan silently added up the number of individuals visible, including those feeding amongst the dotted foliage in the background. The troop size was at least ten in number, including three cuddling young infants. Both males and females look similar. They cannot easily be distinguished, as they have similar morphological features. Interestingly, their newborns are strikingly different in colour. The fur is orange or bright yellow, which changes to grey in six months after birth. It is always fun to watch these small orange balls of fur stuck warmly close to the mother on tree branches, spending their time relaxing, grooming, and searching for food. When I stared into their eyes, the scientifically curious mind of mine asked if there was any rhyme or reason for having such startlingly huge white rings around the eyes besides appearing cute. Primates in general do have larger eyes than many other mammals of comparable body size. But is there any need to make it appear larger by having those rings around the eyes?

On reflection, I remember reading some interesting facts that could level my curiosity. All mammals are divided into those with eyes on the sides of their heads, like chickens, cows, horses; and those with eyes closer together on the front of their faces, like monkeys, tigers, owls, cats, and, of course, humans. What is behind this divide, one might ask? The placement of a pair of eyes from the sides to the front has resulted in a slightly different perspective on what we see in front of us. It allows us to perceive depth. Forward-facing eyes are to give us, including primates, an evolutionary advantage in a number of ways. For primates, this enables them to escape into the trees quickly from their predators.

Furthermore, navigating around the tree branches and leaves in the canopy is made easier with a visual system with good depth perception. The eyes have evolved for us to accurately judge distances. This is especially useful for leaf monkeys leaping from tree to tree living high up in the dense canopy. In short, forward-facing eyes allow these monkeys to see through the dense leaves and branches in their forest habitats. I explained this idea known as 'arboreal locomotion hypothesis' to Stan when we stopped to have a quick lunch of sandwiches we brought along with us on the walk. I asked him to hold up his finger vertically and try focusing his eyes on something far beyond his finger immediately in front of his face.

'Now, do you see you have two copies of your finger?'

'Yes, indeed!' Stan exclaimed.

'But both fingers are perceived as transparent, right?' I asked.

'Wow, amazing. I could see through them.' Stan was totally blown over.

He shook his head, nodding, absolutely impressed with my little demonstration how forward-facing eyes enable us to have an X-ray vision of sort. We are endowed with binocular or stereoscopic vision allowing us to see and judge depth. So for the dusky leaf monkeys, those exaggerated display of their possessing a pair of front-facing eyes isn't just for show but a reminder of how evolution has been kind to them. It has helped them swing and leap in their treetop habitat at fast speed. They are able to see through leaves immediately blocking their vision and make a quick dash to escape from predators. During feeding, they are also able to spot distant fruits and young shoots more efficiently.

Spectacled leaf monkey, a goggle-eyed primate species, once widely distributed across Southeast is increasingly endangered, confined to small fragmented patches of forests including urban areas and commercial plantations.

Owing to its interesting looks, appearance, and adorable size, the dusky leaf monkey or spectacled langur is listed amongst the cutest animals in the world. These cute-looking monkeys are arboreal and spend most of their time on trees. Their natural habitats are quite variable, which may include both forested as well as urban surroundings. Hence, they are encountered in natural forests along the coasts, rivers, lakes, and also urban forests fringing botanical gardens and parks. In the dense forests, they prefer to dwell on tall trees. Being amongst the higher canopies of trees in the forest, they do not have many predators. But they can still be prey for snakes, raptors, and big carnivorous animals that are able to reach them. When found in forests in proximity to urban settlements, they don't seem to shy away from humans. They often come to the lower branches or on the ground, much to the delight of humans trying to feed them with junk food.

Traditionally Dusky langurs are folivores feasting on a wide variety of leaves from their natural rainforest habitats. In recent times however, they have developed an affinity for leaves of plants not usually found in pristine rainforests including exotic species of orchards and plantations. Some would even go for human junk foods.

'They seem to be hungry all the time.' Stan turned to me full of wonder and admiration as he watched the infants clamouring on the mother's back and at the same time grasping leaves from the mother's hand, eating them with gusto.

Balancing Act

The long muscular tail of a dusky langur stands almost perpendicularly as they traverse from tree to tree. The tail serves a similar function to the long pole used in tightrope walking, the skill of walking along a thin wire or rope often performed in the circus. The erect tail swings continually back and forth acting as a counterbalance to the monkey's body weight as it moves at high speed along the slippery narrow branches in the canopy.

'Should we go back to the chalet and get something to feed them?' asked Stan with some concern in his voice. I almost chuckled at Stan's naivety. Typical geologist, I thought. But he brought on a relevant issue here.

Dusky leaf monkeys are primarily folivorous. Their feeding repertoire primarily consists of plant materials, thriving on flowers, shoots, seedlings, leaves, and fruits. Yet primatologists aren't quite sure if feeding them with high-calorie food such as bread and potato chips bought from the regular grocery stores could do harm to them. The negative consequences, if any, of feeding these monkey other than leaves are still an open question. After all, despite urban encroachment, many langurs manage to survive by altering their natural behavioural patterns, including a drastic change in dietary intake.

I'm reminded of Liem's paradox. This is a study done by Dr Karel Liem of Harvard University, who did a study on the feeding behaviour of the cichlid fish, a small Mexican species adapted to eating snails. He showed that the fish would swim right past the snails if it could find softer food. This despite having highly specialised pebble-like teeth perfect for eating the hard-shell snails that are plentiful in their native environment. Liem's paradox suggests that animals can easily be made to avoid the food their bodies had become adapted to eating. This is seen over and over in nature. In the primate world, for instance, gorillas will walk miles past huge supplies of their typical diet of soft stems and leaves to get soft sugary fruits that are harder to reach and require long walks. Monkeys in captivity have been known to avoid fibrous foods like celery if they are offered sugary, fleshy fruits, even though those fruits are harder to digest and not good for them. The same preference might be shown by dusky leaf monkey, preferring Stan's loaf of bread instead of their usual leafy diet.

Daytime, dusky langurs would leave the forests to look for food in locations close to human habitation; but would always return to the tall canopies of the forests for night roosting.

Dusky leaf monkeys consume about two kilograms of food every day whilst weighing only five to nine kilograms. This is possible because of the presence of bacteria in their digestive system that can break down cellulose. The large stomach is divided into various sacs where the upper region is involved in the fermentation of green leaves under anaerobic condition created by cellulose-degrading bacteria. Besides the digestion of cellulose, these bacteria also facilitate the detoxification of the leaves. Feeding them with high-calorie foods like bread, potato chips, etc., might alter the proper functioning of this digestive system uniquely designed by nature. Their physiology and body weight may be adversely affected. But Liem's paradox suggests they might still go for the more tasty urban junk foods and put them in harm's way.

The dusky leaf monkey is diurnal and highly active during daytime. They move around in groups with numbers ranging from five to twenty individuals. Each group consists of two or more adult females and only one dominant male. Like other socially structured primates, the dominant male adult would be responsible for keeping the group together. Patrolling at boundaries of their territories and detecting predators around their territories would be his job. Solitary individuals are also found in both the sexes.

Dusky langurs evolved forward-facing eyes to accurately judge distances while leaping from tree to tree. For this species, the risk is falling and injuring themselves is high if they are not able to gauge instantly the true distance between the branches and neighbouring trees during foraging.

Stan and I were slowly feeling the heat of the day as the rays of the morning sun peeked through the foliage to bathe our bare necks. Almost spontaneously, we spotted a nice shady spot to lean against a tree and rest our legs. An adult female and two juveniles were nearby at visual distances quite aware of our presence. Unperturbed, they continued to indulge with a social play involving chasing, jumping over, wrestling, and pulling each other's tails. We were thoroughly enjoying the circus show before us. When a juvenile wanted to mount on the other, he would have all the four limbs on the ground and cheekily stuck his rump up into the air and made a little wiggle of his rear. As he jumped and scrambled, the mother would be ready to grasp the feet of the mounter in case he missed. Stan was absolutely amused watching the 'come-on looks' on the faces of the playful juveniles as they tried to encourage the mother to join in the fun with no success.

Dusky leaf monkeys communicate through visual, tactile, and vocal communications. Interestingly, these energetic displays of mounting on each other's backs, lunging on each other's heads, and flicking of their tongue at each other are all part of visual communication. The visual communication essentially involves three gestures: mounting, tongue flicks, and lunges. Mounting is thought to be a major way to show domination. The majority of visual communication involves signals that indicate threats to be heeded by those below the hierarchical system.

Tactile communication is an important social behaviour in primates. They touch each other with their fingers and mouths to enhance social bonds, reassure each other, chastise another or indicate status.

As in macaques and other langurs, dusky leaf monkeys also engage in tactile communication, which include social grooming, embracing, grabbing, grappling, and jump kicking. Each of them serves in building and reinforcing the bonds between the individuals. Generally, they show minimal aggression within the groups. They would rather focus on reconciliation whenever conflict arises. Interestingly, this docile and non-aggressive monkey species exhibits ventro-ventro hugging during reconciliation. This means they embrace and hug in belly-to-belly positioning. Just like humans, they would extend and place arms around each other along with kneading each other's fur. This humanlike behaviour is usually involved during consolation and reconciliation. Other tactile communication is employed to express aggression. This involves jump kicking, grappling, wrestling, pulling, and grabbing each other.

Spectacled langurs have polygynous mating system - adult males compete for mating rights amongst themselves. As most primates in the tropics, their breeding season is erratic and reproductive rate is low. Following copulation and fertilization, gestation period is about 145 days with females giving birth once in a couple of years to one to two offspring only.

They also engage in vocal communication involving honking and soft warning calls. Studies revealed that specific noise calls are meant to convey different messages. Adult males honk to demarcate group's territory. A soft warning of intrusion, resembling that of a cough, would indicate the detection of mild disturbance in their territory. But a two-phase noise that characteristically sounds like 'cheng-kong' would indicate a more serious intrusion. When this 'cheng-kong' two-phase noise changes to three- or four-phase noise, that would mean their territory is being dangerously violated and danger is imminent. Other noises believed important in vocal communication of dusky leaf monkeys include squeaks, hoots, snorts, and murmurs. But whether specific messages come with these noises isn't clear.

Newborn of Dusky langurs is orange or bright yellow; strikingly different from adult. This phenomenon known as natal coat coloration allows the mother to notice her baby easier amongst other members of the group.

Not much information is available on the conservation status of the spectacled langur or dusky leaf monkey. They have been categorised under near threatened by the red list category and criteria. The locations of the species have shown extensive urbanisation, and, increasingly, their distributions are getting farther away from primary forests. This undoubtedly is caused by loss of their natural habitats. Besides loss of habitats, urbanisation, and human interventions, they are also hunted down by humans for food in some parts of Asia. Deforestation has significantly depleted their usual sources of food like young leaves and wild fruits. In recent decades, their population in the wild is on the decline faster than ever before. Perhaps this is an indication of their lower reproductive rates, which could be the result of thriving on less nutritious diets unsuitable for herbivorous mammals.

Dusky langurs use their long tail as counterbalance. To remain stable travelling at speed and the heights they normally travel is crucial especially when carrying the young that is clinging precariously to the furs of the mother's chest.

At the foot of the hill, we stopped at a not-too-fancy restaurant for lunch. The atmosphere was strangely still, devoid of any cooling breeze from the sea. The warm and humid tropical ambience seemed to cause some discomfort for my poor guest from Midwest, United States. Sweat trickling from his neck, Stan by now was anxiously eyeing the rows of soft drinks in the coin-operated fridge at the corner of the restaurant. I muttered underneath my breath seeing the restaurant operator taking his own sweet time to attend to us. This despite ours was the only table occupied in the entire food-stall-cum-open-air-restaurant. It was a telling moment. It summed up exactly how people went about their businesses on this lovely island. They basically just went about doing their business whatever suited them. Back in the mainland, such substandard customer service and apathetic attitude would have sunk his entrepreneurial ship before it even set sail. We were finally served with some non-elaborate stir-fried local food, which we both quickly tucked in. I must say, despite their laissez-faire approach to life, people here seemed to cook well. Kudos for that! Making our way back to the hotel, friendly locals were most generous with their smiles as they waved us goodbye. Obviously, the free-wheeling, do-as-we-please attitude seemed to prevail everywhere we went. In fact, it was highly contagious amongst the visitors to this laid-back paradise as well. Within days, strangers were seen smiling and chatting like old acquaintances. No worries.

As we made our way to the resort, I watched the sky growing darker in the distant horizon. We hastily stacked our backpacks under a bushy vegetation nearby in case it suddenly poured. Within minutes, we found ourselves wading in the warmth of turquoise water, soothed by gentle waves around our tired feet. I beamed wide smiles at Stan, who let out a chest-bursting yell, 'How ridiculously perfect this is!' I couldn't help but chuckle in absolute agreement. Very rarely did I end up on an island such as this and couldn't hear myself selfishly moaning about another paradise lost. I would usually lament about overdevelopment, environmental footprints, and unsustainable economy. But Langkawi was somehow different. The tourism industry here had all what it took to steadily grow organically and sustainably. Compared to other premier island destinations in Phuket, Thailand, for instance, Langkawi's speed of development had been relatively slow. Every possible adverse impact on its environment had been kept to a minimal level. Crossing my fingers, I hoped it would stay this way.

After a whole day's outing, we decided to treat ourselves to a sumptuous dinner within the hotel premise. The warm land breeze was blowing out to sea, massaging and soothing my slightly sunburnt neck. I was seriously devouring a perfectly grilled juicy piece of barracuda steak in the company of a friend who also happened to be a highly prolific researcher and writer in the area of geology and earth sciences. But, strangely enough, my mind raced to remember why the wind blew towards land during the day but out towards the sea during the night. 'The land absorbs heat from the sun much faster than the water. During the day, the warm air over the land rises, causing the cooler air from over the water to rush in to replace it. At night, the water cools much more slowly than the land. This causes the warmer air over the water to rise because it is less dense. The cooler air from over the land then rushes out to fill the space above the sea. That is how land breeze is formed,' I could almost hear my old geography teacher at Malay College Kuala Kangsar, Mr Kamalandran, explaining to our form three class almost half a century ago. In my mind, I questioned if my geology professor friend could have explained any clearer. I smiled full of gratitude and salutation to all my old teachers.

Earlier from the cashier's counter, I picked up a glossy promotional brochure featuring Langkawi as a geopark. I learned that on 1 June 2007, Langkawi was officially declared the fifty-second member of the Global Geopark Network under the auspice of UNESCO. A paragraph stated that 'geoparks are nature reserves of unique and great significance with respect to their geological features and biological diversity. By definition, it is a territory encompassing one or more sites of scientific importance, not entirely for geological reasons but also by virtue of its archaeological, ecological or cultural value. Nonetheless, comprising a chain of 99 islands, Langkawi is a mecca for geologists.'

'So what is so special about Langkawi that UNESCO sees it fit to designate the island as a geopark?' I decided it was the right time to pick Stan's brain on the matter at a dinner table conversation.

'I thought you'd never ask,' winking as he took a moment to brush off lingering crumbs of garlic bread from his chops. 'I can only explain as I understood from my own reading. I have not carried out field research on the geology of Langkawi myself, but I am aware of some pertinent studies by a few of my own colleagues at UKM over the years.' Stan undertook to enlighten me on the uniqueness of Langkawi from its geological perspectives.

'Langkawi was where it all began,' he started to explain. 'Two hundred million years ago, the continents of Antarctica, South America, Africa, India, and Australia were joined together as a single supercontinent known as Gondwana, or Gondwanaland. Then clusters of small islands were deposited on the seabed. In this corner of the planet, Langkawi consists of several distinct islands that tell us the most complete geological history all the way to the Paleozoic era. This is the geologic time that began 541 million years ago when marine animals evolved and diversified. Unfortunately, a huge proportion of species on Earth perished about 252 million years ago with the end—Permian extinction, the greatest extinction event in Earth history. Here, amongst the islands of Langkawi, the oldest and tallest would have been Gunung Machinchang. So this mountain represents the earliest part of not only Malaysia but also the entire Southeast Asian region. It can be considered the epicentre or birthplace of this region we came to call Southeast Asia now.'

Mildly surprised, I must congratulate Stan for he had undoubtedly captured my attention. I nodded appreciatively. I could almost feel the enthusiasm building up in my head, especially to finally learn the novelty and geological significance of Langkawi. That marked my first comprehension of the birth of this legendary island and this region Southeast Asia. They all started here with sandstone deposits that grew over millions of years. No wonder Langkawi was also referred to as the foetus of this part of Asia.

I was most grateful to Stan for the 'Geology for Dummies' lesson over just one dinner. Finally, I came to grips with my lifetime ignorance in the area of geology. At last, I really came to appreciate the absolute geological significance of Langkawi, a tropical island renowned not only for its natural beauty and steeped with romantic tales and legendary myths but also for being a living mirror of our geological past. It was a turning point for me. The past three days had taught me to no longer get underwhelmed with rocks. I could now pick up a rock and stop thinking that 'a rock is a rock, is a rock!' but to scholastically hold up in front of my face and say, 'This rock is more than meets the eye. It has heaps of stories to tell that go back hundreds of millions of years ago!' Wow, this island paradise truly rocks!

HAVE THE GUTS TO
FIT FOR PURPOSE

IN 2010, I RETIRED FROM all kinds of formal employment with the universities after close to five decades of wearing different hats as an educator, researcher, administrator, and consultant. But the jobs and roles have always been in the knowledge business. It was then time to spend more quality time with my wife Lesley, children, and grandchildren, who were all in New Zealand, except for my eldest daughter in London. I emigrated to be closer to them and bought a house in Lesley's hometown, Invercargill. Three years into my settling down in a new country, I got an unexpected request to return to Sabah for a job I found it hard to say thanks but no thanks. The offer was as the founding vice chancellor of a spanking new educational entity called University College Sabah Foundation. I've always had a soft spot for Sabah, where I spent thirteen years of my life as an educator and researcher in the 1980s. It was also the most fulfilling phase of my career as an academic. Sabah has been my launching pad in learning and building all I know now about leadership and dealing with difficult people like unscrupulous bosses and politicians. The request to return to Sabah came out of the clear blue sky, but I was stoked to accept the offer. I saw the opportunity as a fresh challenge to complete my unfinished job I was contrived to abandon more than two decades ago.

This time around, I was promised of a clean slate to reboot some of the agendas I felt most relevant to Sabah. In the forefront of my mind was education and research on the state's natural heritage. The next generation must fully appreciate and value their own natural resources and environment. Whilst ensuring progress of economic development, they must become more extroverted to include sustainable exploitation of Sabah's rich and diverse biological treasures. They must do so not at the expense of the environment. Undoubtedly challenging but an achievable feat, I thought. I need to put in place a well-articulated strategic plan for this new institute of higher education to play its roles effectively.

I was raring to go by mid-2013. I started building the university college drawing on Sabah's strength on biodiversity. As a nation, Malaysia is considered one of the thirteen megadiverse countries in the world. Much of this is attributed to the wealth and diversity of plant and animal species found in the rainforests and coral reefs of Sabah. The majestic Mount Kinabalu, reaching an altitude of 4,095 metres above sea level, the highest mountain between the Himalayas and New Guinea, is one of the most scientifically researched mountain in the world.

Covering 75,370 hectares and endowed with a staggering abundance of plant and animal species, Mount Kinabalu Park was declared Malaysia's first World Heritage Site by UNESCO in December 2000. I immediately embarked on leveraging from the wealth of Kinabalu's terrestrial biodiversity. From my previous stints here in the 1980s, I have always felt Sabah people are naturally blessed with creative minds and potentials. This might have resulted from their growing up amongst the wealth of nature and diversity of cultures. I decided to take advantage of these two strengths of Sabah, nature and culture, in educating and training the human capital for Sabah. I ventured to position UCSF as a premier training institution for creative media production, which includes animatics, film-making, videography, and photography.

After a successful pitching effort, I was given a grant by the National Film Corporation Malaysia (FINAS) to produce a film documentary titled

The Guardian of Kinabalu. To ensure the international quality of the production, I engaged a team from the University of Otago, New Zealand, headed by Prof Lloyd Spencer Davis, an award-winning film-maker for his documentary on the penguins of the Antarctica. The team comprising Lloyd, his partner Weibke, and a videographer Robert Brown was keen to undertake the project. Robert's previous vast experience working along Sir David Attenborough would be a huge edge in making this documentary of international quality. For some of the film footages, we needed to travel to Danum Valley, where encounters with wildlife would be more likely especially for tight close-up shots. We took a short flight from Kota Kinabalu to Lahad Datu full of excitement. I was impressed how this once dreary little town on the east coast of Sabah had grown to become quite hectic and buzzing with traffic. There wasn't much difference from any other modern urban towns. It was a gruelling two-hour drive on a 4WD vehicle on unpaved gravel road before we arrived at a plush resort, Borneo Rainforest Lodge, located deep in the rainforests. The journey wasn't as bad as I had warned everyone. In fact, our Kiwi visitors seemed to enjoy the slightly rough-and-tumble journey. All the way they were looking out of the windows, hoping to spot orangutans swinging on trees or pygmy elephants sharing the same road.

In the 1980s, every time I came to Danum Valley, I used to balk at the thought of having to sleep in rooms with no air-conditioning. But not on this trip. The rooms of the resort were fully air-conditioned, and the window and doors were covered with netting. That means I would be able to have a good night's sleep protected from being bitten alive by mosquitoes. I was delightfully relieved and so thankful. After a light dinner, we all had a good night's sleep.

The next morning, after a hearty breakfast at the resort, everyone felt rested and ever ready to dig into the intrepid rainforests. I helped the team with their leech socks. 'Yes, you don't need these in New Zealand. But believe me, here in Borneo, you'd thank me by the end of the day,' I reassured them. The track ahead of us seemed dry and well maintained. I hadn't seen any of those vile blood-thirsty leeches on our path yet.

The visibility was a little blurred by a screen of early morning mist still hanging above our head. All of a sudden, everyone came to a stop. There was definitely some activity up there, a wild rumpus created by something furry within the canopy above. Some branches were swishing and swaying with some orange-coloured creatures within the foliage. Pressing a finger upon his lips, our guide turned to us and almost dramatically whispered, 'There, on the branches there, red leaf monkeys.' Indeed, there were at least six individuals sprinting along the foliage feeding, totally oblivious to our presence. We stopped and stood silently assessing if they were going to be around long enough for some nice shots to film. Robert did manage to get some good footage of these gorgeous animals.

The red leaf monkeys, also known as maroon langurs, is endemic to the island of Borneo, specifically Kalimantan, Indonesia, and Sabah and Sarawak, Malaysia. Found high in the trees, they can survive on primary and secondary lowland forests. Scientifically, the red leaf monkey, *Presbytis rubicunda,* is a member of the family Cercopithecidae. They live in forests at altitudes below 2,000 metres.

Humans invariably identify animals by their colouration. The first thing we learn about nature is that certain animals, especially large iconic mammals, have characteristic fur colours. A giraffe, for instance, has a pattern of interlacing white lines all over its reddish-brown coat; a giant panda is black and white; and a Malayan tapir's front and back portions of their body are black, leaving the midsection white. The maroon or orange-red colour of *Presbytis rubicunda* is similarly quite characteristic for the species. The idiosyncratic curiosity within me asked, 'In general, does colouration play a role in animal survival?' The answer is very much a speculation still. The precise roles of animal colouration are difficult to ascertain beyond any doubt. Research designs are often inadequate. In mammals, including the non-human primates, camouflage appears to be the single most important explanation for the overall colouration. It seems to have been the work of evolutionary force giving the animals a means to avoid predators. The colouration prevents animals from being easily spotted and becoming prey to predatory species. The camouflage enhances their chance of survival in the wild and holds promises for continued existence of the species. It is easy to understand animals can remain concealed when their overall colouration resembles or matches the natural background of their habitat. But how does this work with orange-red colouration of the red leaf monkey? My own spotting of these animals a while ago was made possible because I was distracted by the orange-coloured creatures moving against the deep green backdrop of the canopy. Hardly a camouflage.

Red leaf monkeys are endowed with special sacculated stomachs capable of breaking down tough cellulose from their leafy diet. Hence, they spend most of their picking foliage within the tree canopy above. However, to supplement their diet they do venture to the ground looking for mineral nutrients like magnesium, calcium, phosphorus and potassium, which they get from consuming termite clay or soil.

I posed this question to a graduate student studying camouflage phenomenon in rainforest animals in Danum Valley a few years ago. His response then was an interesting one albeit long-winded. Apparently, camouflage could be achieved in a number of ways. A type of camouflage that we are familiar with is called crypsis in which the overall body colour blends with that of the habitat. We see this often in insects and reptiles. The second type of concealment is known as obliterative shading. Instead of blending in the environment, this type of concealment is achieved through disruptive colouration. The contrasting colours or irregular markings on the animals serve to break up their body outline, making them hard to be detectable by predators. The third type of concealment is by having their underside lighter coloured from the rest of their body. This serves to counteract the sun's glaring effects when the sun is shining from above. In the case of red leaf monkey, I was made to understand it could be all the three types of concealment in operation. It is anyone's guess which one of the three types of concealment works the best for a bright-orange ball of fur leaping and swinging against a lush green rainforest backdrop. All that remains vaguely clear.

Red leaf monkey is a strict folivore, meaning an herbivore that specialises in eating leaves. They are therefore referred to as colobines—animals that are able to live exclusively on leaves, and their digestion process is in multichambered stomachs. On occasions, they would feed on flowers. They sometimes combine consumption of young leaves with flowers to extract proteins not commonly found in mature leaves. Fruits and seeds would also complement their diet with additional concentrations of fats and carbohydrates. The feeding patterns of red leaf monkeys vary with seasons. In the rainforests, fruit season peaks during June to September, when an increased production of fruits would be there for the asking. During this time of abundance, they would stuff themselves with large amounts of seeds and fruits. Consumption of young leaves primarily happened from October to June. Rainforests, despite the name, do have dry seasons when rain doesn't occur as often. During this dry time of the year, red leaf monkeys would resort to consuming more succulent foliage and decreasing their intake of seeds. When food becomes scarce, they would even feed on mature leaves usually untouched during good times.

To conserve energy and contend with the humid tropical heat of the rainforest, Red leaf monkeys spend much of the daylight hours sleeping or resting. They seem to favour taking naps on exposed branches high up in the canopy for more breeze to cool their body down.

In terms of preference, red leaf monkeys spend around half their time eating leafy greens and the other half eating seeds and fruits. Leaves are favoured because of their high fibre content, and their digestive system is highly equipped to handle food digestion of plant origin high in cellulose content. As a microbiologist, I've often been asked to explain how the three-chambered stomach of animals like cows, cattle, leaf monkeys, and other ruminant animals help to break down the consumed leaves. A common feature in all these ruminants is having large stomachs that are divided into chambers or sacs. The large size allows slow passage of a large quantity of leaves. The huge amount of leaves in the stomachs can constitute as much as a quarter of the animal's body weight. Despite the high content of hard-to-digest cellulose, folivores like red leaf monkey completely digest what they consume. This is made possible through the aid of microbes found residing in their stomach. Here, the cellulose are efficiently broken down into fatty acids through anaerobic fermentation. This occurs in the upper part of the stomach. The stomach microbes also help to detoxify chemicals such as alkaloids found in plants. These microbes, however, are very sensitive to changes in pH levels in the stomach. So to avoid bellyaches, the animals would consume huge amounts of seeds as well to neutralise the acidity in their tummy. On occasions, they would venture to the ground and feed on termite clay for the mineral nutrients. Termite mounds have high concentration of organic matter and nutrients such as calcium, magnesium, potassium, and phosphorus. Consuming termite soil helps to relieve acidosis of the stomach as well as supplements their diet that contains scarce essential nutrients.

Compared to other primates, red leaf monkeys are almost strictly arboreal. They spend most of their time in the canopy. It is interesting to shed light on the disproportionate amount of time red leaf monkey spend in relation to the types of food they consume. In a study carried out in Danum Valley, Sabah, it was observed the red leaf monkeys spent 46 per cent of their feeding time on young leaves, 38 per cent on seeds, 12 per cent on whole fruits, 2 per cent on flowers, 1 per cent on bark, and 1.2 per cent on pith. These feeding duration would change with inclement weather conditions such as drought or forest fires. Field data such as above would be potentially useful to gauge the reliance of red leaf monkey on different food resources. It can help us to fall back on evaluating their population in times of food shortages. For example, conservation efforts can be based on monitoring how the scarcity of leaves within the habitat could have affected their population in certain habitats.

Red Leaf monkeys spends almost 60 percent of each day feeding on leafy greens, seeds and fruits because they can digest the cellulose and fibre contents in such diet quite efficiently. Fruits and seeds provide them the fats and carbohydrates required for the energy to be expended and stored.

But from where I was standing, I could also see some individuals on the ground. So red leaf monkey aren't strictly arboreal. They seemed to be busy feeding on something. I pored through my binoculars and discovered they were putting something in their mouths that didn't look like leaves or any other plant matter. Upon straining my eyes, I then realised they were converging on a patch of termite mounds and busy stuffing something into their mouths. Mystery solved! These monkeys were feeding on the topsoil of the termite nests found protruding erect from the forest floor. That didn't surprise me at all because I happened to know a thing or two about animals eating soils. A few years ago, there was an English student doing research on this subject at Danum Valley. I learned from him about the science of this phenomenon called geophagy.

Despite being herbivores feeding primarily on leaves, seeds, and fruits, they can tolerate a slight change in the menu. They may be selective feeders, but they can only behave so when surplus of food is available. Certain types of plant matter or seeds can become scarce at times, even in the lush rainforests of Borneo. What can they do then to remain physically active and physiologically healthy? They still need to maintain a balance in their diet. It is during such period that red leaf monkeys have been observed to consume topsoil from termite mounds. Strangely enough, as they eat the termite mounds, they would leave the termites alone. Why such bizarre behaviour? They are actually after the minerals needed to balance their diet, not the termites. By eating the soil, they could maintain the balance of minerals in their body because topsoil of termite mounds happen to be a good source of potassium and phosphorus.

One might ask, why topsoil of termite mounds rather than the soil on the forest floor? This question has been somewhat answered. The reason they eat topsoil of termite mounds rather than the soil around them had something to do with the saliva of the termites secreted during the process of nest building. During the construction of the mounds, the topsoil is contaminated with termite's saliva, known to be rich in minerals and enzymes. Besides proteins from the saliva, the topsoil enveloping the termite mound contains high levels of calcium and magnesium. The soil is also known to be highly acidic because of the high aluminium content. Functionally, highly leached aluminium is proven to be efficient in the exchanging of cations in our body physiology. To date, the consensus has been geophagy amongst non-human primates is a behaviour in times of mineral deficiencies. But our knowledge on geophagy is far from complete.

Red leaf monkeys have a uni-male social system consisting one adult male, one or more adult females, juveniles and infants. Upon reaching adolescence, males of this prenatal group would eventually leave to travel on their own or join an all-male group before finding females they could form a uni-male group.

The deliberate consumption of soil, dirt, or even rock is also observed in several herbivorous and omnivorous mammals. Geophagy has been the subject of in-depth research for decades not only in primates but also in a wide variety of vertebrates, including, but not limited to, ungulates, elephants, tapirs, bats, and parrots. The causes and consequences of this behaviour across all taxa remain poorly understood. Geophagy is especially widespread amongst non-human primates. There might be other reasons besides maintaining a balanced diet. Recently, it has been suggested that some primates may use geophagy to combat intestinal problems, particularly diarrhoea. The commonality amongst earth consumed by these animals is the presence of clay minerals. This is hardly surprising as humans have used the clay mineral kaolinite for centuries as the primary active ingredient in antidiarrhoeal.

The next morning, I suggested to the filming crew we visit the suspended walkway built by the Borneo Rainforest Lodge. It spans 300 metres long and hangs about 30 metres high above the forest canopy. That would definitely offer a different perspective into the rainforest. Furthermore, that would be a great opportunity to spot some of more than 340 bird species that dwell high in the canopy. Different types of epiphytes rarely seen below have also been reported growing beyond our reach within the canopy. Perhaps the crew would strike the opportune time of obtaining close-up shots to reveal the intricate details of orchids, aroids, lichens, mosses, and ferns found growing up there.

We had a marvellous experience going on the canopy walkway. I was cautiously observing if anyone amongst the four of us was feeling anxious because of excessive fear of heights. Thank goodness no one suffered from acrophobia. It was breathtaking and simply awesome to be amongst the richest biomes on planet Earth. Dubbed as the 'high frontier', the rainforest canopy represents an extra-special zone where millions of species coexist, including epiphytes, lianas, bromeliads, mammals, birds, frogs, ants, and beetles. And, believe it or not, even earthworms have been seen way up forty to fifty metres above ground where not a speck of 'earth' was found.

This is not at all surprising because the tropical rainforest canopy has been of interest to some of the greatest biologists for nearly two centuries. Since 1815, Alexander von Humboldt described the treetops of the Amazon as a 'forest above a forest'. Even Alfred Russel Wallace, the famous British naturalist, explorer, geographer, anthropologist, and biologist who independently conceived and published the theory of evolution with Charles Darwin, was impressed. He proposed the theory of evolution by natural selection after making an expedition to the Amazon and was immediately blown away by the immensity of arboreal biodiversity high up in the treetops. In 1842, Wallace wrote, 'A few forest trees were also in blossom; and it was a truly magnificent sight to behold a great tree covered with one mass of flowers, and to hear the distant hum of millions of insects gathering together to enjoy the honeyed feast. But all is out of reach of the curious and admiring naturalist.' William Beebe spent years exploring the flora and fauna of Guyana sailing gently in a balloon over the canopy layer. In 1917, he wrote, 'Yet another continent of life remains to be discovered, not upon the Earth, but one or two hundred feet above it, extending over thousands of square miles.' As expected, the filming crew wasn't disappointed. We were totally gobsmacked with what we saw up there. Everyone was greatly enjoying the view below as we took our own sweet time filming and cautiously traversed the walkway. The filming crew got to have a bird's-eye view of the vastness of the rainforest canopy. They were pleased with many invaluable tight shots of epiphytic plants and insects found flourishing up above that otherwise would have gone unknown to the vast majority of documentary viewers.

The evening was cool and pleasant. Beyond our netted windows, a musical repertoire was in full swing. Almost every sound imaginable emanated from the pitch darkness of the rainforest. The cicadas whined to no end. Crickets too seemed to join the chorus. They stridulated by rubbing their upper and lower parts of the wings together, creating chirping sounds. Frogs croaked at premeditated and purposive intervals. Tokay geckos barking almost desperately for mates. Nightjars whistling. Owls hooting. All in combination, they came out as a soothing melodic ensemble in the darkness. Ironically, these were the same sounds that used to freak me out as a child coming from my father's orchard behind our village house. Inexplicable sounds that would make me swiftly draw my blanket over my head petrified. But my Kiwi friends seemed more curious than terrified of these strange noises. In the shower back at the resort, I had a little surprise. Despite the leech socks tightly wrapped around my legs from the knees down, I discovered a veritable 'army' of leeches feasting on my thighs and calves. How they managed to sneak up beats me. I related this little drama at dinner, which made everyone break into a hearty chuckle. They appeared calm and found my leech story humorous. But I could see the sudden change in their faces as they were laughing—perhaps a tad unnerved thinking if they had checked every possible parts of their own body in the shower before dinner.

The film production team was pleased with an extremely fruitful trip to Danum Valley. Some valuable footage was obtained fulfilling the purpose of the journey deep into the virgin rainforests of Danum Valley. They spent an additional two weeks filming around Mount Kinabalu Park, including the summit of the mountain, before flying home. The completion of the documentary film took a few more months for the post-production phase, which included editing of footage and arranging them into a complete narrative. Finally, the documentary *The Guardian of Kinabalu* was ready.

It is a story about a native of Borneo named Alim Biun. To the Kadazandusun people, Mount Kinabalu is a sacred place—the revered abode for the spirits of the dead. On 5 June 2015, this sacrosanct home of the spirits was damaged by an earthquake. Eighteen people were killed by a massive landslide that followed. Six days before the earthquake, ten Western tourists stripped and urinated on top of the mountain. The despicable act, the locals believe, has angered the spirits at the sacred mountain. It is a violation of the local belief and ethos. At the same time, deforestation and pillaging of natural resources are occurring at unprecedented rates. Many known and unknown species of plants and animals are driven to the brink of extinction. Alim sees the urgency of protecting Mount Kinabalu. This couldn't be more ominous as the mountain becomes increasingly popular with its status as the World Heritage Site in 2000. Since leaving school, Alim never has any doubt of what he wants to do. Born at the foot of the mountain, he learns how to venerate Mount Kinabalu as expected of his Kadazandusun ancestry. Exceptionally virtuous as it sounds, Alim has been playing his part in protecting the sanctity of Kinabalu. To him, this comes as naturally as breathing the crisp fresh mountain air around him. He makes it his calling to educate the younger generation about this hugely prominent and significant ecosystem. Some people just feel the rain, but Alim gets wet. He doesn't just become enamoured with the mesmerising beauty of Kinabalu Park where he works. Alim also invests heavily on his passion to learn, understand, and love all the plants and animals he sees around him. Soon he becomes a beacon of light to many nature lovers around him. They view him with adoration. His is in a rarefied league of his own. This is the story of Alim, the guardian of Kinabalu. This fifty-two-minute documentary film won the Special Jury Award at the Eleventh Kuala Lumpur Eco-Film Festival, held at Black Box, Publika, in Malaysia on 27 October 2018.

THE PUNK WITH SILVER LINING

WHEN I WAS OFFERED THE position of the deputy vice chancellor of University Malaysia Sarawak in 1994, I wasn't in two minds about it. I finally got the opportunity to live in Sarawak, the other Malaysian state in Borneo Island. It was a dream I've been quietly entertaining in my head after having served in Sabah. My thirteen-year stint in Sabah, after all, had proven to be my most riveting and prolific period in my career as an academician. I've explored most of the rainforests and corals reefs in Sabah. But I've not seen much of the peat swamp areas Sarawak is famous for. I have always fancied understanding more about the tropical wetlands including mangroves and peat forests with all their equally unique flora and fauna.

The lowland peat swamp ecosystems are well represented in Sarawak. Its organic soils known as histosol have developed only within the past 5,000 years, a recent phenomenon in terms of geological process. But its unique ecological features make peat swamp areas home for a host of unique plants and animals. They are also richly endowed with threatened species that require further studies and documentation. Their close proximity to premier locations in coastal areas also make peat swamps highly sought after for human settlements. They are worthwhile investments for housing and industry developers. Peat swamps can be owned at cheaper price, drained and reclaimed for individual bungalows or seaside resorts. Wise stewardship and sustainable development of this ecosystem are crucial. Ecological information on peat areas is urgently needed to put in place conservation policies and best management practices for peat swamp conservation. My new position and ensuing roles as the deputy vice chancellor in charge of research fitted like a glove.

Clouds of mist clung to the face of the peat forest at dawn. A convoluted network of streams fed the shallow patches of water bodies found haphazardly across the entire swamp. This pristine wetland was targeted for the development of a huge resort complex as part of the Sarawak ecotourism industry. A team of researchers from my university was tasked to carry out an environmental impact assessment (EIA) study before the project could be given the green light to start. I was the project leader of the study and immediately realised how daunting the task would be. The panoramic vision of the lush greenery reflected on the numerous blotches of water bodies told me so. There were towering trees projecting out amongst thick clusters of thorny pandanus vegetation. But the natural ambience was pristine and peaceful. A perfect getaway refuge for nature enthusiasts but definitely not an easy natural habitat to study and produce a well-judged and fair environmental impact assessment. Exercising prudence is the key.

This unique peat swamp ecosystem is widely known for the habitation and proliferation of a diversity of wetland and aquatic life. Some of us in the team have been here before. They told us of their rare encounters with a dazzling array of both terrestrial and aquatic wildlife including monkeys, otters, frogs, and snakes in the peat swamp. Not necessarily found in abundance, but they are often unique for this type of wetland. The draining and land reclamation of this wetland could essentially drown most of the natural habitats for these creatures.

We started the task with meeting the people living within the proximity of the area under study. This wasn't just customary and respectful but also most useful in the process of getting as much local knowledge as possible. We would attempt to gain some clues as to the exact whereabouts of the wildlife populations from the local villagers who seemed to be most hospitable and welcoming. They were more than happy to assist. Some readily volunteered information on where to go to see animals they had themselves encountered inadvertently since living in the area.

As we were noting down the possible species of mammals they had come across in the area, a few youths were excitedly trying to tell us about the existence of a type of monkey they termed 'Monyet Bekam'. None of us had ever heard of a monkey with such name previously. We thought that could be just another name of a monkey we were familiar with but referred to in their provincial dialect. We shook our heads in confusion trying to figure out which monkey or ape they were calling Monyet Bekam. After much guesswork and confusion, one of the boys came up from swimming in the river nearby and approached the group. He noted the confusion and put an end to the puzzlement. He spruced up his wet hair into a Mohawk hairstyle and started kicking the grass blades like a football player. Almost spontaneously, all of us jumped up, exclaiming, 'But, of course, the silvered leaf monkeys. Monyet Bekam is Monyet Beckham, David Beckham of Manchester United!' We all had a hearty laugh. By then, the boys were also laughing, nodding non-stop. I jokingly said they should be proud of the fact that punk hairstyles of the European subculture were actually inspired by their neighbours, the silvered leaf monkeys. I asked them who they think made the hairstyle famous, David Beckham or their neighbours? You can guess what their answer would be, of course. Besides the uniquely in vogue punky single spike on the head, silvered leaf monkeys also don bushy crests of silvery grey furs that sprouted across the middle of the skull from both cheeks. This Old World monkey gave you that special feel—lovable and cheeky all in one!

With a pair of blood shot eyes staring out from their silvery black face and hairs sweeping upward into a point, this genteel and unusually human-friendly Silvery leaf monkey is often monikered as the rainforest punk.

We knew of the occurrence of silvered leaf monkeys in this area from past visits and journal publications by foreign scientists. Silvered leaf monkeys, also known as silvery lutung or silvery langur, are found in coastal mangroves and riverine forests in Peninsular Malaysia, Sumatra, and Borneo. As recently as 2008, the presence of two subspecies of silvery langurs has been suggested—namely, *Trachypithecus cristatus cristatus,* found in Borneo, Sumatra, and Natuna Islands; and *Trachypithecus cristatus selangorensis,* found only in the Peninsular Malaysia.

They are specialist folivores; meaning, a major portion of their diet includes leaves. They do eat fruits, seeds, and flowers too, but 80 per cent of their diet are leaves. They are able to even feed on mature leaves considered too tough and unsuitable for consumption by other species of primates. Like other langurs, silvered leaf monkeys are well adapted for arboreal life. They are suitably endowed with a large three-chambered stomach similar to that of cattle and other ruminants, allowing complete digestion and fermentation of the cellulose found in their herbivorous diet. They have also evolved a set of teeth with grinding ridges so that tough leaves and fibrous shoots can be chewed and processed more efficiently. This is probably the reason why silvery langurs are usually found in different parts of the forests quite apart from other monkey species. Even if they are found within the same forest areas, the silvery langurs tend to be found feeding in the middle canopy of the forests. The branches of the higher trees are usually left for other species to feed; usually monkeys with frugivorous diet. The silver leaf monkeys seem to be happy to let other monkeys to enjoy the more luscious fruits found in abundance on the upper canopy whilst they feed on the more fibrous leaves below. A sharing and coexisting attitude that can be a guiding principle for our behaviour perhaps?

In their natural habitats, silvered langurs live as a community. They travel in search of food in groups of fifteen to twenty-five individuals. Their social structure is definitely that of male dominance. They live much like in a harem of one adult male and numerous females. Each troop would be closely guarded from others within the community by an alpha male, who overbearingly takes charge. He will provide protection to all females in the troop and keep vigilant against other males or possible predators. Infants also travel with the group to be taken care of by the females. The females remain loyal and stick around in the group for life, whilst males would leave not long after reaching maturity. They would join other groups of male monkeys until they are able to form their own harem.

The face of a Red leaf monkeys can range from bluish to black in colour and the body is covered with unmistakeable shaggy reddish-orange coat that tends to get lighter around the stomach. A pair of big dark eyes and a deep jaw might give one an impression of a mean and ferocious monkey which can't further from the truth. It is however a shy and unapproachable creature by nature.

Silently I studied a few individuals that had ventured closer to meet us. I was pretty sure they were curious to find out what our business could be intruding into their domicile. Outwardly, adult silvery langurs possess a combination of fearsome as well as comical appearance. Their faces are covered with lush silvery grey hairs forming a pointed crest on top of the head, making them appear strikingly formidable. Yet their haphazardly pointed hairs around the cheeks, each strand almost standing on ends, prompt you to question if the animals are constantly exposed to static electricity fields. From within this dark-grey face, a pair of huge bloodshot eyes were staring out at me. The long fixated hollow gaze was spine-chilling, making me feel uncomfortable. But somehow the surrounding atmosphere seemed calm and peaceful. They weren't boisterous and unruly at all. Unlike other monkey cousins that could be intimidating and nerve-wracking in the face of human intrusion, silvery leaf monkeys seemed more docile. They would hang around humans, watching us expressionless, just as questioning as we were watching them. At the same time, they would be nonchalantly busy grooming and playing with other members of the group. Focusing on bonding amongst themselves seemed to take priority than bothering about human presence in their midst.

Red leaf monkey also consume a range of forest fruits and seeds especially when there is a short supply of young shoot after bouts of dry seasons. The species plays an important ecological role in dispersing seeds and help in the regeneration of its forest ecosystem.

Flaunting their spiky Mohawk hairstyle, these monkeys looked like a gang of punks on the city streets of Amsterdam. Their underlying demeanour seemed similar too. They symbolised rebelliousness in a docile fashion. They seemed to not care about authoritarianism or anarchy and just like to go about in their own ways.

At that moment in time, I felt there was nothing more wonderful than seeing Mother Nature in her purest forms. It was an absolute joy to see a few-month-old baby clinging to the mother effortlessly. The baby seemed to be born endowed with unusually strong grip for holding on to the mother. Since birth, a young infant was born with striking bright-orange fur except for white hairless skin on the face, hands, and feet. Within days of being born, their white skins turned black like the adults. Then it took around three to five months for the infant's fur to turn silvery grey like an adult, beginning with the head, slowly transitioning to silvery grey from where this species got its name.

While traveling through the trees, Silvery leaf brachiates by swinging their arms from limb to limb often in the company of an infant. But when walking on the ground or climbing through the trees, they do so quadrupedally on all four feet.

My eyes became fixated at the gorgeous colour of the infant clinging to the mother's chest. I wondered, under what circumstance would such bright orange colour would be of any good to the baby besides looking cute and cuddly? Scientists have given several reasons why the baby is strikingly coloured. Three interesting theories have been put forth. Firstly, the babies' bright-orange colour would make it easier for mothers to spot their young in the forest when they go astray. Secondly, the orange colour of infants is a form of extraordinary camouflage, since they would be more vulnerable to lurking predators. Thirdly, the orange colour would make identification within the group easier to encourage alloparenting.

Let's look at these three theories separately. The first theory is pretty straightforward. Bright orange invariably tends to spring out noticeably from amongst the green foliage of forest trees. The second theory is also plausible, although it appears contradictory to the first. On one hand, the first theory is based on the contrasting property of the orange colour.

On the other hand, the second theory is based on the camouflaging property of the orange colour. That doesn't make sense to me. Pondering deeper, though, it just might hold water. In the wild, silvery langurs are preyed upon by wild cats such as tigers and leopards. Most of these mammalian predators are known to be red or green colour blind. Cats by nature possess fewer photoreceptor cells or cones in their retinas compared to humans. Consequently, cats are able to see fewer colours akin to a colour-blind human. They can only see shades of blue and green, but colours like reds, pinks, and orange are confusing to cats. Hence, strikingly bright orange can factually serve to offer effective camouflage to infants of silvery langurs.

The third theory seems conceivable as well. Silvery langurs, like all Old World monkeys, are by nature trichromatic; meaning, they can see red, green, and blue like humans. Hence, they would be able to easily identify the orange-coloured infant against the dark-grey colour of adult coats. This can effectively serve to remind adult monkeys to take care of their young infants in the group at all times. Raising the young is a communal responsibility in the world of silvery leaf monkeys. Besides the mother, other females in the troop would also lend a hand in caring for the young especially after the biological mother stops lactating. I learned this through first-hand observation. At one point, I was startled to see another monkey 'snatching' a baby from the arms of another monkey obviously busy cuddling the infant. I was expecting a big fight over this. On the contrary, the mother seemed to tolerate this 'abduction' of her baby. I was naturally flabbergasted by the mother's attitude until I saw the 'baby snatcher' suckling the baby on another branch close to the mother. The mother by now had gone about on her own way foraging for more leaves to feed herself. Special care of their natural mothers seemed irrelevant to the babies of silvery langurs. Raising infants is a genuinely collaborative responsibility.

Breeding season is marked by the visible presence of bright orange infant in stark contrast to dark grey chest of mother. Newborn has orange hair, white hands, feet, and face. In a couple of days of birth an infant's face turns black and body hairs change to adult colouration within 3 to 5 months

Such parenting behaviour is termed alloparenting, where individuals other than the parents would provide care for the infant. It is more like communal nursing, which can also include babysitting, carrying, and feeding. In the monkey world, alloparenting is deemed to increase reproductive success by providing more protection from predators. It is believed to also inculcate and nurture social development of infants. In the process, alloparenting can help future parents to learn mothering skills before raising one of their own. This reminds me of a metaphor I heard from my housemate, a Kenyan student, John Kamau, when I was studying in New Zealand, 'It takes a village to raise a child.' It is a proverb from Nigerian Ibko culture about shared responsibility. Everyone has a role to play, and there's a place for everyone. Not only parents play an important part in growing a child, but also so do the neighbour and the entire community. I was left entirely gobsmacked at the thought these langurs had caught on to such an important and effective concept of shared parenting.

The acidic environment of peat swamps is known to support unique species of plants and animals. Sphagnum or peat moss grows well here and can gradually fill a size comparable to that of a massive lake. This lowly plant can contribute significantly in our effort to address climate change issues. When the peat moss invades new areas, it produces large amounts of hydroxide that makes the environment extremely acidic. Such condition prevents dead plant matters found in the environment from decomposing. Without decomposition, the carbon remains stored in layers upon layers of dead plants instead of being released to the atmosphere in the form of carbon dioxide. Over years, colossal amount of mosses continually and ultimately sink to the bottom and create peat deposits that act as carbon sink. The conservation of peat moss, therefore, would be of great consequence. Draining and burning of peat swamps would only help in releasing immense amounts of carbon dioxide and methane, the two greenhouse gases primarily blamed for powering global warming. Leaving these huge areas of Sarawak peat swamps alone would definitely be one of the recommendations to be included in our EIA report. We need to attach more importance to peat swamps on the same level we have accorded to other wetlands in Malaysia such as the mangroves, lakes, and rivers. It would be another crucial step forward in conserving huge areas of carbon sink and methane reserves. It would be Sarawak's gift to the world community in doing its part to save planet Earth from global warming and climate change.

Hornbills show special affinity for **pristine** lowland tropical **rainforest** areas with an abundant supply of fruiting trees. Their presence is generally a reliable indicator of the health of a forest.

Above against the cloudy sky, my eyes followed the elegant flights of a pair of pied hornbills. These gracious hornbills are most adored for their unusual 'double-storied bill'. Sarawak holds a special place for visitors wanting to catch a glimpse of these giant birds. Housing eight out of the world's fifty-four species, Sarawak deserves the term of endearment 'the Land of the Hornbills'. Whilst the sky above will always be there for these magnificent feathered beauties, I was troubled by the draining of the peat swamps that has been happening at unprecedented pace in recent years. All in the name of development and economic progress, peat swamps have been rendered dry through land reclamation for housing and plantations. This wetland ecosystem is no longer suitable for many animal species requiring aquatic environment to breed. I wonder how many species of frogs and fishes are yet to be discovered in this area. In 2011, an old friend of mine, Prof Indraneil Das, was stoked beyond belief to have rediscovered a toad thought to have gone extinct since 1924. This is *Ansonia latidisca*, commonly called the Bornean rainbow toad. A diminutive stunning toad only to be found in the moist tropical rainforest and rivers of Borneo was last seen in its natural habitat more than ninety years ago. Today, it is ranked as the top most wanted lost frogs. Many herpetologists have listed the rainbow toad as having gone extinct forever. But during one of the night trips into the mountainous terrains of Sarawak rainforests, my friend Neil proved that extinction need not be forever for all species that we no longer see today. It isn't forever. High up in the Penrissen mountain range, the supposedly extinct rainbow toad was still thriving well and safe. Three individuals were spotted in three separate trees: adult male, adult female, and a juvenile. Measuring not exceeding 5.1 centimetres in length and possessing flamboyant multicoloured slender limbs, this rainbow toad is a phenomenal treasure. Simply gorgeous. To an internationally renowned herpetologist Neil, this was like discovering a living *Tyrannosaurus rex*. Undoubtedly, such gem would have a strong demand in the illegal wildlife trade. It could fetch a hugely handsome price amongst amphibian collectors around the world. Fearing there could be a mad rush to poach these awesome creatures from their natural habitat, Prof Neil Das is keeping the exact location of this species close to his chest. Wonder how many more such supposedly extinct species are found here in this peat swamp in front of me? It has been most neglected by scientists because of the difficulty in accessing soggy and unwieldy conditions.

The Bornean rainbow toad was last seen 87 years ago in 1924. Listed as one of the world's top 10 most wanted frogs, the chances of spotting this mysterious long-legged toad was nil until it was rediscovered by scientist in Penrissen, Sarawak in 2011. The exact site of the discovery is not disclosed for fear of poaching due to the huge demand for brightly-coloured amphibians as pets; amongst which Bornean rainbow toad is second to none.

In recent years, there has been a worrying trend in the seriously declining populations of frogs worldwide. About ninety frog species have gone extinct in the past fifty years. It is traced down to a deadly chytrid fungus that has been killing frogs globally. Chytrid fungus causes an infectious disease called chytridiomycosis in amphibians. Humans, other mammals, reptiles, birds, fish, and invertebrates are not affected. Frogs are infected through their thin moist skin used to absorb water and balance the levels of sodium, chloride, and potassium inside. Once infected, the frog is unable to maintain a steady heartbeat and will die of a heart attack. In the last five decades, the populations of more than 500 amphibian species are believed to have declined because of chytrid infections. You may ask, why do we need to be concerned about this massive die-offs of frogs? I can't overemphasise the fact that frogs play an important role in the food chain. Frogs are both prey and predators. As prey, frogs play an immense role in nature. They are an important source of food for a host of animals, including birds, fish, monkeys, and snakes. As predators, they assume a critical role by eating insect pests and disease vectors. Without frogs, humanity will suffer the most. Our agricultural produce and food production would significantly decline. More worryingly is the spread of vector-borne diseases. Deadly diseases like malaria and dengue are bound to continue, causing carnage in the tropics without the help of frogs making wholesome meals of the mosquitoes.

Not only do 'wasteland' and 'wetland' rhyme, but also in Malaysia these two terms are often seen as synonymous by policymakers, politicians, and industrial leaders. They fail to value the two as important ecosystems capable of bringing non-tangible benefits to humankind. We need not repeat our past mistakes with respect to recognising the value of our wetlands. It took human loss and suffering of immense magnitude before we came to realise the importance of our mangrove wetlands, for instance. The undersea earthquake of 26 December 2004 off the coast of Sumatra caused a series of tsunamis that unleashed untold damage and destruction on the coastal regions surrounding the Indian Ocean. It was only then that the protective role of coastal mangroves against the destructive forces of tsunami became apparent. Those lowly plants could have saved thousands of lives! It was shown that coastlines fringed by mangroves were far less damaged than those where mangroves were absent or had been removed. Mangrove forests shield coastlines by reducing wave amplitude and energy. Only now, the mangroves, once looked upon as no-good mosquito-infested wasteland, is highly considered worthy of conservation. I would like to see such change of heart towards peat swamps too. Their pivotal roles in relation to climate change have not been long ignored in Malaysia.

Ten days of toiling in the peat swamp have been most rewarding. Observing and identifying plants and animals living in this oft-disregarded ecosystem have succeeded in reinforcing our team's belief in the need to leave it alone. We must not shut our eyes to the future plights of species found to thrive here. We were totally washed out, exhausted. Our bodies may be exhausted, but our minds are fresh with ideas on what to write in our EIA report to the state government. After having a much clearer picture of the peat swamp ecosystem in general, we would come up with conservation strategies and mitigation measures to ensure the biological functions and biodiversity are not adversely affected. If at all the targeted land area is to be drained, reclaimed, and developed for building construction, a prudent management program must be put in place. That must not be done at the expense of the plethora of unique flora and fauna associated with the peat swamp ecosystem. In particular, the future plights of silvered leaf monkeys and the important roles of peat moss in climate change must be amply discussed in our EIA report. We must be mindful that future generations only have us to blame for not having the strength of minds to do something about loss of biodiversity and climate change.

AGILITY AND GRACE AT DIZZYING HEIGHTS

The only way in and out of Tawau Hills Park was through a long stretch of unpaved road of gravels and laterite clay only passable with a 4WD vehicle. On both sides of the road, I noticed the immense spread of oil palm plantations interspersed with cocoa plantations, a new commercial crop introduced to this rural district in recent years. The volcanic soil of this area was found to be highly suitable for cocoa growing. Stepping out of our air-conditioned transport, we found ourselves in the familiar humid surrounding of the Bornean tropical rainforest again. Not just the greenery and magnificent vista around, the place even felt and smelt familiar. I was sufficiently acquainted with this lowland rainforest reserve when I used to accompany Datuk Lamri Ali, the director of Sabah Parks, on many occasions previously. Upon our arrival, a park ranger gave a quick briefing on the accommodation facilities and accessible forest trails in Tawau Hills Park. It was a short and useful briefing but long enough to make everyone drenched in sweat standing and listening in that hot and humid atmosphere. This typically happened in minutes for just being within the proximity of a tropical rainforest. We made our way to the quaint wooden cabins in the park ground. Everyone was pleased to learn the facilities were running on generators, which meant we would be able to charge our mobile phones and stay connected. That was a big deal nowadays; unlike in the 1980s, when every visitor to this park had to be contented with ATUR, the only wireless telephone system available. Even then, it was only for use in urgent situations. There was no Wi-Fi, though. At least we knew for the next few days, we wouldn't be completely isolated from rest of the world. Some of us have started to prepare our meals using a gas cooker to heat up the canned sardines bought earlier.

Whilst waiting for dinner to be ready, our guide offered to take us on a night walk into the depth of the rainforest. Equipped with knee-high Wellington boots, headlamps, and anti-bug spray, we headed out on a narrow trail into the pitch darkness of the forest. We treaded cautiously avoiding the puddles and criss-crossing exposed roots on the soaked ground. The evening was buzzing with insects, frog calls, and reticent creatures intent only to be heard not seen. This was the real rainforest, an absolutely surreal experience that couldn't be captured in words or pictures. We encountered a few interesting frogs, geckos, and spiders along the trail. At one point, we found an opening to the sky amongst the silhouettes of canopies move. The guide asked us to stop and turn off all torches on our foreheads. Instantaneously came into view one of the most unforgettable skyscapes I had ever seen. The sky above was glittering with millions of stars. All around in that pitch-black setting came sighs, whimpers, grunts, or growls, whatever you wanted to call them. Everyone was totally electrified with what they saw above. Simply magical.

A rewarding night walk indeed. We spent a good forty minutes looking for red eyes along the trail. Most turned out to be reflective red eyes of spiders, but some lizards and frogs too. In time, everyone was feeling tired and hungry, ready to head back. At the lodge, we were happy to be in the glare of light bulbs again. The electricity generators ran only for a couple of hours in the evening, and lights out came by midnight. That gave us enough time to get through dinner. The constant sweating took a while getting used to especially after meals. Even after taking a cold shower, the sweltering heat and 96 per cent humidity could be testing. Fortunately, our cabin came with a few hammocks, our go-to respite after dinner. Before calling it an early night, I shielded ourselves from the flying creepy crawlies with the mosquito nets provided.

The best part of the day in the tropical rainforest was early morning. Amidst distant calls of the gibbons from deep in the valleys, fogs drifted through the still air. The sun climbed slowly sending smoky rays streaming through tree trunks and branches. Bands of clouds, big and small, bathed the many layers of the rainforest. Just like the early birds chirping merrily as the clouds appeared to float across the forest canopy, I was also an early riser compared to the rest of the crew on this trip. Almost every one of the entire film crew was still deep in their clumber. I was here to help produce a film documentary titled *Into the Wild of Sabah, Borneo,* in collaboration with an film production company based in Paris.

It was only drizzling when we set off for the filming trip that morning. Peering through the gaps of the forest canopy, I could see black clouds rapidly forming above. From a distance, the drowning sounds of the tropical rain was sweeping through the foliage and gathering speed, threatening to completely drench all of us below. Like a hermit crab frantically looking for a shell, everyone scurried around looking for shelter. The crew wasn't the least worried about getting themselves wet, but it'd be a disaster if our cameras and all the filming accessories got doused. Such scenarios had been all too familiar often encountered during filming in the rainforests. Rain could be non-seasonal here, happening at any month of the year, any hour of the day. We had to stop for lunch anyway. The filming crew decided to take shelter and grab a bite of the sardine sandwiches before they too got drenched. Everyone seemed happy just to peel the plastic cling wrap off their sandwiches and catch a duly needed breather after the hurried walk. As we were settling down having bites off our lunch pack, suddenly an unusually heavy shower of rain poured upon us. It came right from above us. Worried about our filming equipment, we instantly looked up. Something just swung past within the canopy. It disappeared in a distance as quickly as we became aware of its presence. We couldn't make out what it was until one of the park rangers reassured us that it was the agile gibbon *Hylobates agilis.*

Designed for Performance

The elongated forelimbs, hands, and feet of a gibbon are as useful and practical as they come. They are adaptations for brachiation, the primary mode of travel through forest canopies for this creature. Lar gibbons do not have tails and therefore can't use tails for counterbalancing when traversing within the canopy like langurs do in remarkable fashion. But evolutionary process has proportionately produced the perfect design of its limbs for use in locomotion. Gibbons are able to move about swiftly and safely amongst the rainforest trees towering forty to fifty metres in height.

Gibbons are the least closely related to man of all apes. The smallest of all apes, there are nine gibbon species found throughout Southeast Asia: the agile or black-handed gibbon (*Hylobates agilis*), the Bornean gibbon (*Hylobates muelleri*), the white-handed gibbon (*Hylobates lar*), and the black-furred siamang (*Symphalangus syndactylus*). In terms of ecology and behaviour, they are all very similar, with the exception of siamang, which is nearly twice as heavy as the others. Agile gibbons have smaller territories and feed mainly on leaves. Also known as the black-handed gibbons, they are inhabitants of the lowland dipterocarp forests of Sumatra, Malaysia, and southern Thailand. Light and mobile arboreal apes, agile gibbons possess slender bodies, long arms, and no tail. Their fur varies from very dark brown to a light buff, with white hands, feet, and brows. Male agile gibbons can be distinguished from the females by their striking white cheeks. Their thumbs are not attached to the palms, like human hands, but joined at the wrist. Agile gibbons are omnivores. Their diet includes mostly fruits, leaves, and insects. Their specialised thumbs, detached from their palms, allow more flexible movement in securely holding to tree branches, reaching and picking hanging fruits, and grabbing crawling worms and caterpillars.

I swiftly trained my binoculars towards the direction of its path. It was jaw-dropping to see a huge lanky and furry brown thing moving gracefully within the branches and foliage of trees. The animal wasn't more than twenty metres away from us by then. Still poring through my rangefinder binoculars, it seemed to have made a U-turn heading back towards us in a flash, not even stopping on its track. It was a wonder to watch as they effortlessly stretched their long arms, swinging from branch to branch, transporting themselves in an incredible speed. They were brachiating—a manner of arboreal locomotion primates are adept in by swinging from branch to branch employing only their extra-long arms. Swinging up to three metres and leaping more than nine metres, this form of locomotion allows rapid and direct reach for food sources in the canopy. Swift agility in movement also helps them to protect their large territories from neighbouring troops, which they declare by hooting voices that could be heard several kilometres away. They warn others about the presence of predators in the same but perhaps in a more specific hooting voices. Their home territory usually covers about twenty-five hectares, which is equivalent to thirty football fields. They would defend their domains from neighbouring families usually by displays and songs that can carry over several kilometres into the gullies and valleys of the rainforests.

Agile gibbons are monogamous species despite living largely as sociable animals. Monogamy or pair-living involves a male shield and care for a single female instead of searching for additional opportunities to mate with other females. The female feels protected against infanticide of her progeny by other males.

It wasn't only their mode of locomotion that impressed me about gibbons as a family of apes. All gibbons live in stringently guarded territory. They are fanatical in the manner they defend their own domain, brandishing robust visual displays and haunting songs. Visitors to the rainforests are often woken up in the early morning by their long loud calls heard echoing from the valleys throughout the upper canopy. Gibbons are strictly monogamous and territorial. They live in small family groups, each consisting of a single breeding pair and their offspring. Each group has its own area of the forest. After dawn, the forest rings with their songs. The males sing around dawn, and towards later morning, duets are sung by the adult pair. The most spectacular song of all comes from the female gibbon. Every morning, soon after sunrise, the female would perform her 'great call'—a loud shrill wail that invariably rises to a long drawn-out crescendo, filling the morning air for fifteen minutes or more. Each female's call stimulates her neighbours to reply, so that waves of sound float across the treetops of the rainforest. Some sing for hours with a series of rising and falling notes. At the climax of her song, she trills—singing loudly in a series of quickly repeated high notes. She would sometimes do this running up and down branches, grabbing and breaking off leaves. Her call tells other female gibbons nearby to keep away from her mate. Their repeated bouts of singing are often duets announcing their claim to a home territory. In marking or defending their territories, male agile gibbons also give out calls that can be heard over several kilometres. Their songs are duly recognised by other neighbouring families, which will stay clear of the valleys or canopies from where the calls originate. This vocal warnings are almost always respected and heeded by other individuals found in the same valleys. Potential intruders should know to stay clear. Failing to comply to those warning calls could see both male and female gibbons resorting to physical and visual displays of defence. On most occasions, that would succeed in scaring and chasing the intruders away.

Gibbons are fanatical at defending their territory. They would do this with a flurry of visual gestures and vocalizations as if they are about to snap and hurt the intruder. But judging the temperament of gibbons can be difficult. When resting, their facial expression conveys as if they are worried, sad or preoccupied.

Gibbons are the champions of swing. They are one of the most arboreal of the primates. They are designed to be so akin to having 'four hands' rather than two feet and two hands. Its rapid movements and great agility make gibbons the 'unequalled' king of the canopy. With their long arms, they can propel themselves through the forests by swinging from branch to branch with great agility and speed. The agile gibbon is reputed to be so acrobatic and fast that it has been known to catch birds on the swing. In one swing, most gibbon species can travel a distance of nine metres easily. This is often observed with a baby confidently clinging to the mother's chest. But to give her infant extra support whilst she is swinging through the trees, the mother would impulsively fold up her legs to form a kind of cradle. The comfort and safety of the baby seem to take precedence as well.

Despite being almost uncompromisingly arboreal, gibbons do occasionally descend to the ground, where they usually walk upright on two legs with their long arms outstretched. It is a funny sight to watch them doing so. They would be holding their long arms above their heads like someone doing a boogie-woogie on a dance floor. A flashback came to my head. I was in Thailand attending an international conference on medicinal plants in 1984, and as part of the post-conference tour, participants had the opportunity to visit the National Zoo in Bangkok. I was with another conference participant from the United States watching the gibbons kept on land enclosures where gibbons could roam freely but unable to cross the moats built surrounding the man-made islands. It was another memorable monkey moment for me. That was the first time I noticed the inexplicably weird way gibbons walked. I jokingly remarked that the gibbons couldn't stand their own smelly armpits in the sweltering heat. They were airing the stink out by raising and waving both hands above and walking around. My American friend turned around smiling at me, unsure if I was seriously ignorant or was I just trying to be funny. That was the moment I learned from him the reason why gibbons always walk on the ground with hands waving above their head was to keep his balance. They would be balancing in a similar fashion walking on big tree branches in the canopy. Gibbons use their exceptionally long arms much like a wire walker uses a long pole for balance. The advantage in this technique lies in the basic physics pertaining to the law of inertia. The use of the pole, in this case the long arms of the gibbons, distributes the body mass away from the pivot point, thereby increasing the moment of inertia, which is fundamental in balancing our movement forward. It is true that you learn something every day if you care to pay attention to small details.

Gibbons and Old World monkeys have ischial callosities, commonly referred to as sitting pads. These are tough, bony padding on their buttocks that enable tailless primates to sit on thin branches comfortably and for longer duration during feeding.

As with all gibbon species of the rainforests, the social structure of agile gibbons comprises serially monogamous pairs. They remain mates for life and sing a duet every day to strengthen their bond. Every pair's call is unique to them. The female seems to exhibit more devotion—exhibiting loyalty and commitment to a monogamous family arrangement. The mother gives birth to a single offspring after seven months' gestation. She would nurse and care for her young till about two years of age. When fully mature at about eight years, the offspring would eventually leave the family group in search of a mating partner. This further perpetuates the monogamous lifestyle of a gibbon. Their offspring end up living in the upper canopy of the rainforest, feasting on fruits, leaves, and insects, but only rarely would they venture to the ground.

Vision in Position

Evolution has placed the two eyes of primates in the frontal position instead of on each side of the head like birds. This is the product of primate evolution 55 million years ago at the beginning of the Eocene epoch. It gives them increased binocular vision of what's ahead of them. Living amidst thick foliage and branches within the canopy, primates like gibbons need to perceive greater field of depth to judge distances when they are on the move. Such stereoscopic vision comes in handy when looking for food or avoiding predators.

On hindsight, I found the next stretch of trail notoriously hilly. The terrain was perhaps a tad too challenging to beat with a full stomach. By then, I was tired and soaked with perspiration. My calf muscles were sore, and I noticed my sheen was bleeding from a leech bite. 'So that blood-sucking creature did manage to get me after all,' I conceded defeat this time around. The day had grown hotter, and the air was unbearably humid. The chorus of crickets and cicadas was completely muted by now. Even the chatty chirpings of birds seemed to have mellowed.

The film crew decided to push ahead and find a good vantage point to get panoramic footage of the valleys below. It would be great to give the viewers of the documentary an expansive bird's-eye view of Tawau Hills Park, almost 300 square kilometres of primary lowland and hill forests. We walked along an uphill trail towards Bukit Tawau, the highest peak within the park. Hopefully, such spectacular shot showing the immensity of protected rainforests could make viewers understand why Tawau Hills Park was reputedly rich and diverse in their faunal biodiversity. Somewhere hidden within that carpet of greenery were mammals, birds, reptiles, and amphibians of which a high percentage were endemic, found nowhere else in the world. It was our intention to make this documentary most compelling in presenting the urgency to protect and conserve the biodiversity of Borneo and Sabah would show the way.

By now, the atmosphere along the trail was relatively voiceless and muted. The morning air at this higher elevation seemed fresher and cooler as we continued huffing and puffing ascending. Then a breathtaking view greeted us. A jaw-dropping panorama of rolling hills and mountains unravelled before us. Towards the pale distant horizon, there was a white veil of soft white clouds from which magnificent crowns of only the tallest of trees emerged triumphantly. The valleys and ridges were alive. Familiar sounds of the rainforest reverberated through the green valleys. Gibbons whooped to their hearts' content, announcing their exclusive territories. Geckos barked to solicit attention of their mates. The brown barbets repeated their trut-trut calls without a pause from high up, totally hidden behind the thick foliage of the canopies. Cicadas incessantly whined at ear-piercing pitch. Too early to be calling for mates at this hour of the day, I thought.

As the mist slowly lifted, I found myself asking a little enigmatic specific of nature, 'Where do these clouds and mists come from?'

I was told since school days that fog, mist, and clouds are formed when water vapour condenses on soluble particles found floating in the air. Fog, mist, and clouds are but droplets of water formed during overnight condensation. These liquid droplets, however, need airborne particles to manifest themselves as what we call fog, mist, or clouds. My next question is 'Where do the particles come from to become concentrated in the valleys of a rainforest?' It has long been assumed that most aerosol particles above the rainforest consist of organic materials formed through chemical reactions of gas molecules in the atmosphere. Volatile hydrocarbons such as isoprene are released from plants, which consequently become aerosol particles and act as seed particles for the formation of fog, mist, or cloud. Recently, however, a group of scientists showed this notion was only partially accurate. The most important of these particles turned out to be potassium salts, not just organic particles. They were surprised to find very high potassium levels in the aerosol samples collected early in the morning. They also found these potassium salts are metabolic products of mainly fungi and plants of the rainforest. Subsequently, the potassium metabolites are released and become suspended in the air between valleys of hills and mountains. Here, they serve as condensation nuclei to which the organic molecules adsorbed. Hence, fungi and plants directly influence the formation process of fog, mist, or cloud in the rainforest. The amount of aerosol particles in the air determines the formation and composition of mist, clouds, and precipitation in the rainforest. And the amount of aerosol particles is determined by the concentration of potassium metabolites produced by fungi and plants.

This recent discovery should help scientists identify and quantify the sources of organic aerosol particles in the rainforests. They can now focus more on the biological components known to directly release potassium salts into the atmosphere such as fungi and plants. More importantly, I thought, this could potentially provide insights on the role of lower plants like fungi in the formation of clouds and precipitation.

Understanding this would explain how rainforests affect rainfalls and our microclimate. Ultimately, this would lead to that much-awaited understanding of how deforestation and loss of biodiversity could influence global warming and climate change.

Whether you are a first-time or returning visitor to this Tawau Hills Park conservation area, you would be filled with optimism by the end of your trip here. You would feel rewarded as you have witnessed a lush emerald-green panorama of a 60-million-year-old living treasure. You would have encountered and been overwhelmed with the enormous variety of life forms found here. But let your experience here leave you with a cautious optimism as well. Looming in the horizon are yet serious threats facing these tropical species of the rainforests. Agile gibbons are today listed as endangered on the IUCN Red List. This shy primate species is hugely popular as pets. Illegal pet and wildlife trading is a lucrative and big-scale business internationally. Agile gibbons are particularly sought after because they come in a range of colours—black, brown, light tan, and reddish brown. Both males and females possess white eyebrows. However, only males have white eyebrows and cheeks. Today, aided by the relentless destruction of their habitats, populations of agile gibbons in the wild are rapidly shrinking. The forests within Tawau Hills Parks may be pristine and adequately protected, but this reserve is currently surrounded on all sides by a sea of oil palm plantations. Tawau Hills Park is essentially an 'island' that limits the movement of its local wildlife populations. This would affect the natural distribution of species because they can't travel long distances in search of food and new territory. A far-reaching potential problem here is their genetic diversity. Confined to restricted small habitats, agile gibbons would be drawn to interbreed within their already small populations, resulting in genetically weak offspring. That in itself would be disastrous with a strong likelihood of pushing the species to extinction.

We can tell a lot from someone sitting with their arms folded. It can have a variety of meanings - feeling anxious, resistant, tense, insecure, afraid or responding to distress, A person also crosses his arms in an attempt to "block out" what he is hearing. But for gibbons, it could as well be a gesture of prayer requesting we stop destroying and diminishing their natural habitats.

Surrounded by thousands of hectares of oil palm plantations, a more immediate problem for agile gibbons of Tawau Hills Park is human-wildlife conflicts. For food, wildlife in the reserve, including gibbons, tends to venture outside their normal habitats to find food. In doing so, they would be seen by the oil palm industry as crop pests that need to be eliminated. Poisoning and hunting of wildlife around Tawau Hills Park have seen an increase in recent years. Wildlife animals are trapped and killed. Urgently needed are forest corridors connecting Tawau Hills Park with other conservation areas that can be used by animals to move from one suitable habitat to another in search of food. Without these connectivity, wildlife would constantly be in the way of human economic activities. Human-wildlife conflicts would only increase, casting a grim future for large- and medium-sized mammalian species of the rainforests, including elephants, primates, wild boars, honey bears, and deer.

As we travelled back to the Lahad Datu Airport to catch our flight back to Kota Kinabalu, everyone's desire to explore, discover, and film the varied ecosystems, plants, and animals unique to this part of Sabah was very much satiated. Pleasantly stupefied, the crew had captured all the sagacity of wonderment of our precious rainforests. The subdued light streaking through the canopy layer; the countless different shapes and colours of leaves, flowers, stems, trunks, and climbers; the grand ensemble of forest sounds and shrilling calls of creatures would have been all captured on films, leaving behind, however, the constant freshness of scents in the humid mid-air of the rainforests emitted from the decomposing leaves and plant debris on the forest floor. In the heads of our filming crew, those lingering smells would be stored only in olfactory memory—the recollection and persistence of odours only neuroscientists could comprehend. I took a deep breath and gave myself some time to tune in to the new milieus and surrounds of the urban environment again. I have thoroughly enjoyed the brief moments witnessing the most agile and graceful creature of the rainforests, the dark-handed gibbon, *Hylobates agilis*.

MAESTRO TRAPEZE OF
THE RAINFOREST

IN THE LAST THIRTY-EIGHT YEARS of my life as a university
lecturer and administrator, I have primarily lived in Sabah and Sarawak,
the two Malaysian states on the island of Borneo. Understandably, my
vision and understanding about tropical rainforests have been scanty
and incomplete, only limited and partial to that of the Bornean flora
and fauna. Back in Peninsular Malaysia, I felt this zealous craving to
open up and savour the fabulous flora and fauna of the Taman Negara
in Pahang. I have heard as much as necessary about this 4,343-square-
kilometre expanse of virgin rainforests, internationally hailed as the
gem of Malaysia's nature reserves. My insatiable curiosity was replete.
The most satisfying thing to do would be to venture there for myself.

Arguably, Malaysia's Taman Negara is one of the world's oldest rainforests.
It has continued undisturbed and remained unspoiled for at least 130
million years; meaning, it is older than either the famous Amazon or
the Congo rainforests. This vast expanse of pristine lowland rainforests,
covering a total area of 4,343 square kilometres, represents the most
important protected area in the Peninsular Malaysia. Its iconic images
of massive tree trunks leaning precariously over the river in a feat to get
the most sunlight has attracted hundreds of thousands of tourists from
all across the globe. I have always wanted to be looking up from a boat

at those towering dipterocarp trees lining the riverbanks at remarkable angles. In places, these huge trees have crashed into the river, and the trunks can be seen festooned with hundreds of species of epiphytic ferns, mosses, and orchids. These fallen trees provide opportunities for nature photographers to take great close-up images of epiphytes otherwise thriving beyond our reach way up above. An awe-inspiring spectacle of a magnificent pristine rainforests unique to Taman Negara.

Finally, I got the much-awaited chance to visit this oldest tropical rainforest in the world on a business trip. I was invited to give a series of lectures on rainforest biodiversity to a group of park rangers as part of their career development programs. The cool quaint chalets of Hilton Hotel offered a great night's sleep after hours of sitting still on an extended two-hour journey by a long wooden boat that afternoon. I was very much looking forward to stomping the forest trails the next day. The prospect looked good too according to the weather report. Enraptured despite my having little faith in the Malaysian weather forecast.

One thing to expect of a rainforest forest is rain. In bed, I heard echoes of thunders thumping and rumbling accompanying sudden flashes of lightnings. Fiery glistening threads cracked, splitting the blackness of the night sky. Torrents of rain followed soon after. Within minutes, the forest was drenched and soggy. By morning, the rain had stopped. The forest appeared greener with little puffs of mist floating through it. I was anxiously waiting for the boat that was to take us to a spot along the riverbank where we would start our walk into the forest. To kill time, I ventured along the bank of Sungai Tahan with my steaming binoculars pressed against my eyes. A pair of pied hornbills was trailing each other from tree to tree. I was intrigued by what I saw—how a virtually top-heavy bird, fronted with huge casque and bills, could possibly maintain its balance in flight with such grace and beauty.

The wilderness and wonders of Taman Negara were to be revealed by morning light. The meandering Sungai Tahan with its emerald-green water greeted us like no other rainforests I have seen in Borneo. Against a backdrop of multilayered shades of green hills, the river glittered in the mid-morning sun. I immediately felt the peace and tranquillity often associated with the sheer calmness and beauty of a riverine setting. The sheer number of plant species simply amazed me. They provide shelter and food for a multiplicity of wild animals here. Amongst the undergrowth, the verdant green covers were sporadically interrupted by brightly coloured flowers adapted to attract the profusion of forest insects. Epiphytes such as orchids, lichens, mosses, and ferns were found everywhere—on the branches, the trunks, and even the leaves. Climbing lianas, woody stems of varying shapes and lengths, were seen drooping from various heights. They overhung across the waterways in every possible direction, seeking for the most direct way to reach for the sun. I found myself disbelieving the fact that these lianas and prickly rattans began life on the forest floor and have climbed up towards the sunlight for survival, all racing upwards clamouring for the rays of the glorious sun. The colossal complexity of things in the rainforest was simply unfathomable.

As the boat throttled past sleepy villages on the riverbanks, happy and convivial folks and children waved welcomingly. We pulled in along a small stretch of muddy riverbank. I hopped off the boat clumsily, not forgetting to grab my camera case along. My bare feet sank slowly in the rocky dirt path leading towards the jungle track we were supposed to be taking for the next few hours. Everyone looked for a dry spot to re-attire themselves with trekking shoes and leech socks they took off before alighting the boat minutes ago. Soon, everyone was silently treading the track silently and carefully. It was almost impossible not to stumble over the massive network of roots on the ground. 'What are these roots doing exposed on the forest floor? Why didn't they get deeper into the ground and extract all the good nutrients to feed these enormous trees?' I annoyingly queried. There is, however, a good reason for huge rainforest trees to do that. Despite the luxuriant growth and lush green appearance of the rainforest, the soils here are actually very impoverished. All the nutrients available for these growing trees are largely found only at the surface level, not deep underneath. Because of this, rainforest trees have evolved to form very shallow roots that creep along the forest floors in search of nutrients, sometimes hundreds of feet away from their trunks. These extended roots increase the area over which nutrients can be absorbed from the soil. The shallowness of these roots makes the parent tree very prone to being blown over by strong winds and tropical storms. Very tall tree species with huge crowns develop ways of avoiding this. They are strengthened and stabilised by forming buttressed roots. These strong support roots grow out from the base of the trunk sometimes as high as fifteen feet above ground.

Buttress roots provide strength and stability to massive top-heavy rainforest trees from being blown over and unrooted by gusts of strong winds over the years

Suddenly, we heard repetitious calls of the wild echoing from the valleys not too distant ahead. We instantly recognised the uniquely familiar call of the white-handed gibbons, *Hylobates lar*, an endangered primate in the gibbon family, Hylobatidae. They live in small family groups, each consisting of a single breeding pair and their offspring. Their social organisation is dominated by monogamous family pairs, with one breeding male and one female along with their offspring. Being strictly monogamous, they need to be very territorial too. When a juvenile reaches sexual maturity, it would be expelled from the family unit. They sleep sitting up in trees with bent knees and faces buried between the knees and chest. This way they are always ready to jump into action whenever an intruder violates their territory. For bonding between monogamous pair, they would sing duets with the male and female complementing each other's part. These duets not only help the couple to bond but announce their territory at the same time. The calls are repeated over and over, clearly hoping they would be listened and heeded to by other inhabitants of the valley. We all stopped and strained our ears to fully appreciate their efforts and persistence. It, however, needed specially trained ears of primatologists to tell exactly what the calls meant. To my ears, the song was just a wild melody from the valleys yonder but could have meant more than that to the primate experts. Mating proposals or desperate stress calls perhaps?

There are five species of gibbons, also known as small apes, found in Malaysia. Of all the apes, gibbons are the least closely related to man. The white-handed gibbons represent the smallest of all apes in the Malaysian rainforest. Altogether, there are nine gibbon species throughout Southeast Asia, but only four are commonly encountered, including the agile or dark-handed gibbon (*Hylobates agilis*), the Bornean gibbon (*Hylobates muelleri)*, the white-handed gibbon (*Hylobates lar*), and the black siamang (*Hylobates syndactylus*). In terms of ecology and behaviour, they are all very similar, with the exception of siamang, which is nearly twice as heavy as the others and has smaller territories. In terms of species distribution, the white-handed gibbon, dark-handed or agile gibbon, and the siamang are found in Peninsular Malaysia, whilst Muller's gibbon and Abbott's grey gibbon live in Sabah and Sarawak. Primatologists could tell which species from their calls.

Gibbons have disproportionately long arms equipped with sturdy rotary cup shoulder joints that allow them to raise their arms straight up above their heads without much restriction or difficulty. This ability helps them to brachiate with ease and swiftly at great momentum

There exists a recognisable call that characterise *Hylobates lar*. The species could be easily identified even if you have heard it once or twice previously. They are known to emit short hoots followed by more complex hoots. But the call invariably starts with unsteady quivering sound, followed with regular intermittent hoots that sound smoother and longer. They would continue hooting for several rounds and close with short bouts of quivering sounds again. Characteristic calls can be relied on to determine species differences amongst the gibbons of the rainforests. Recent studies indicated that gibbon songs have evolved as means of communication in dealing with conflicts within the species. They declare territories by hooting. Family groups inhabiting a firm territory would protect and ward off other gibbons with their calls. Each morning, the family would gather on the edge of its territory and begin to sing a 'great call.' This is, however, primarily a duet between the breeding pairs. They would also warn other individuals, especially infants, about the presence of predators through hooting. The hoots might differ slightly for different signals. In the presence of lurking predators like tigers, clouded leopards, crested serpent eagles, and reticulated pythons, their hoots tend to contain sharp higher-pitched reverberations than normal calls.

Gibbons call early in the morning to mark their territory or get mate attraction. The male and female sing a duet in harmony but individually singing a different song. More human-like, the vocal tract and larynx resonate independently allowing amplification of the lowest-pitched sounds differently from the highest-pitched

White-handed gibbons have soft white fur on the upper sides of their hands and feet from which their name was derived. Like all gibbons, they are tailless apes living high up in the canopies of the rainforests. Famously hailed as the fastest of all primates, they travel so fast, they barely touch a branch before swinging off and grabbing the next branch. They are known to 'fly' up to forty feet through the air and leap long distances before landing. This earned themselves the moniker the maestro trapeze of the rainforest. Their extraordinarily long arms gave them the superb ability to swing effortlessly amongst the tree branches. This ability is called brachiating. With their hooked hands, they can move swiftly with great momentum, swinging from the branches. Hence, they spend most of their life within the canopy and very rarely descend to the ground unless they have to.

Within the canopy, they are enthralling to watch. White-handed gibbons are known to be able to suddenly change direction in a split second. I have seen video evidence showing this gibbon species catching birds in mid-air only to eat them upon landing on tree branches. A miraculous feat indeed. Sometimes the species would push this gift of nature a little too far. Gibbons have been documented to have accidental falls. Not for lack of their supple and agile abilities, but small or rotting branches that failed to withstand the weight of this creature causing such rare accidents. But mishaps do occur resulting in gibbons suffering from bone fractures in the wild.

I tried to guesstimate the length on each leap it was making. A mother gibbon I was intensely observing could have easily covered a distance of nine metres with just a single swing. I cringed at the sight as she was confidently executing this giant leap with an infant precariously clinging to the mother's hairy chest. But even the infant looked confident and seemed to enjoy the ride as well. Notwithstanding, you just can't fault her parenting gentility and etiquette. I found it amazing to watch how a mother gibbon candidly and naturally cared to give her baby the extra safety and comfort during travel. Whilst she was swinging through the trees, the mother pulled up her legs to form a kind of cradle around her baby, securing the safety of travel to another level.

This acrobatic prowess of white-handed gibbons also comes handy when crossing rivers or large openings in the forests. It enables them to cover large areas of the rainforest in search of food. I walked towards the direction of the calls. Through my binoculars, I spotted one sitting on a branch seemingly feeding and 'singing' at the same time. It rose up and walked in search of more leaves. As it increased the speed to a run along the branches, it held both arms high in the air. From where I stood, it almost looked like a furry human figure quite ready to slip off the branch and fall to the ground. But he seemed to be skilfully grabbing leaves and putting them in the mouth at the same time. A memorable occasion came across my mind. I was presenting a scientific paper at an international conference on medicinal plants in Thailand in late 1980s. As part of the post-conference tour, participants had the opportunity to visit the National Zoo in Bangkok. I can still recall a conversation I had with a participant from the United Kingdom there. I casually asked him why the gibbon we were both watching then was walking with both its arms waving above its head. I jokingly presumed it either had one too many pints to drink or just couldn't stand its own smelly armpits and doing the best to air the smell out by raising both arms in the air. The guy looked at me most perplexed, not knowing if I was seriously ignorant or just joking. That was the first time I learned that gibbons walk the way they do to keep their balance using their long arms much like a wire walker using a pole for balance. The advantage in this technique lies in the basic physics pertaining to the law of inertia. The use of the pole, in this case the long arms of the gibbons, distributes the body mass away from the pivot point, thereby increasing the moment of inertia, which is fundamental in balancing our movement forward.

In any case, gibbons are bipedal. Just like humans and birds, apes walk on their two limbs albeit occasionally. We walk bipedally without having to adjust the posture of our body. But some apes like the chimpanzees walk with their knees bent and their backs sloping forward. This creates better balance for walking. Most big-sized mammals are quadrupedal, using all their four limbs to walk. Compared to quadrupedal mammals of same body mass, animals that walk on two legs use less energy. This mode of moving around is more economical and advantageous because we don't have to waste extra metabolic energy in carrying out our activities.

A galloping flier travelling through the canopy at break-neck speed exceeding 50 km per hr is bound to accidentally crash down and literally break its bones. This could happen when gibbons grow to a size big enough to power their jumps but their weight is too heavy to be swinging from smaller branches.

It wasn't long ago that white-handed gibbons were hunted for their meat. But I have read no reports of this practice of late anywhere in the regions it used to be widespread. But young gibbons are still trapped and sold in the pet trade in some countries, particularly Thailand. At least that was what I saw during my visit to the famous Chatuchak Weekend Market in Bangkok. It is the largest open market like no other with more than 15,000 stalls and 11,505 vendors selling almost anything under the sun including wildlife as pets. *Hylobates lar* are almost white at birth and develop their final adult colour at two to four years old. It is one of the better-known gibbons often kept in captivity because the species survive reasonably well in captivity. Their white fur on the upper sides of the hands and feet are nice and soft, making them so cuddly and appealing as human pets. I have seen private individuals keeping *Hylobates lar* as pets when I was in Bangkok in the 1970s. I was made to understand this strange diversion can still be found amongst the wealthy people in Thailand, though not as openly and widespread now. Gibbons are usually kept in artificial wire mesh enclosures big enough for the animal to swing about. Even in captivity, they would elegantly propel themselves with great pace and agility in mid-air using their long arms fully stretched. Somehow, this entertains their human masters. Laugh out loud.

Assignment of species conservation status means little in many parts of Borneo and Southeast Asia countries. While keeping primates in captivity in many parts of the world is trending towards a thing of the past, it is still common to see legally protected species kept as pets in Indonesia, Thailand and Malaysia. They are traded openly at weekend markets in large cities targeting rich affluent people.

The fur colour of Lar gibbons may vary from black, dark-brown to light-brown, but their hands and feet are invariably white. Similarly the unmistakable ring of hair that surrounds their black face is always white. Both males and females can assume any variation of brown colour making identification of gibbons gender based on colour unreliable.

Geologically, Taman Negara was sited on a vast expanse of sedimentary rock, periodically scattered with intrusions of huge granites and limestone outcrops. Many millions of years ago, almost the entire land mass of today's Malaysia was submerged under water. Over eons of eruptions, buckling and unfolding of this terra firma, the Earth's crusts were pushed up and islands were formed. Out of this, Peninsular Malaysia emerged during the Jurassic era. This was amply substantiated by the presence of fossilised remains of animal or plant life preserved from an earlier era in the sedimentary rocks of Taman Negara. Fossil records showed that the forests of Southeast Asia have existed in more or less their present form for 70 to 100 million years. Awestruck, my mind froze at the thought that these forests in Taman Negara have been around ever since dinosaurs roamed the Earth.

I gave my all to triumph over an unusually precipitous crest of a hill. A ridge of some sort, it must be the highest part of the forest we have reached that morning, I thought in between my short, quick breaths. I was absolutely drenched with perspiration. I sat down to catch a breath, and again, everything seemed so close. The rugged outcrop on which I was sitting, the tall trees above and further down the slope, and other mountains on the horizon, they all were but one huge peace haven. Nature's tranquillity ruled supreme here. I decided to take a breather and spent several minutes looking around. The morning felt humid but thank goodness breezy. I stopped and looked closely at the trees and underlying bushes, focusing on their shape and beauty. The luxuriant ever-green foliage unselfishly participated in the gas exchanges, which provide much of the world's oxygen supply.

I struggled uphill with astute determination, grabbing tree trunks. By now, I was extra cautious placing my forward tired foot on protruding roots and stumps along my trail. Huffing and puffing, I found a cool spot on a huge granitic boulder, sat cross-legged, and savoured the euphoria. I was struck by the closeness of the purple hills in the distance, or at least I felt that way. The same perception applied to the few puffs of white clouds drifting overhead. I felt as if I could reach out and touch them with my hand. I wanted to stay here forever. The day was brilliant with sunshine and blue sky. The trail we took was a loop that took us to another part of Sungai Tahan bank where a boat was waiting to take us back to our resort. I couldn't be happier because I was truly ready to call it a day by then.

Back at the resort that evening, no one could conceal their hearty approval learning that a barbeque dinner has being prepared by the hotel chef. The aroma coming from the grilled steaks, chicken wings, freshwater prawns, and fish turned us into drooling fools. The outdoor space was beautifully lit with spotlights at strategic places to reveal the majesty of trees around the hotel compound. Standing erect before me, I recognised the famous strangler fig. This magnificent plant started life as an epiphyte high up on tree trunks and branches. The seeds were carried up there by birds and monkeys that fed on the fig fruits. The seed germinated, and soon its seedlings began sending down long roots to the ground. Here, it became well nourished, feeding and growing on the rich nutrients found in the topsoil of the forest floor. As it grew, the host became surrounded by more roots from above. Over time, the seedling quickly grew into a full-blown tree huge enough to eventually suffocate and kill the host tree. From where I was sitting, I could see the enormous hollow core of an upright strangler fig; all that was left of the original host tree. A relationship where friends became foes in the fight for survival in the rainforest.

I contented myself with a good selection of meat and vegetables on my plate and looked around for an empty seat amongst the big round tables nicely set by the hotel. I decided to find an ally to share my excitement on my first day encounters at Taman Negara. I found myself sitting next to a middle-aged tourist getting started on her dinner. I casually extended a 'Selamat Datang' welcome to her—a touch of Malaysian hospitality. Her name is Lesley and hails from New Zealand, a very chatty kind of character and had been touring the country on her own. She had been to a number of interesting places including a few Malaysian rainforest and beaches I have not heard of. It didn't take long for two nature lovers to find ourselves delving passionately into a series of green issues.

Clearly impressed with what she had seen so far, Lesley wanted to know if Malaysians are in general concerned about environmental issues such as global warming, deforestation, biodiversity, and species extinction. Hmm, one of those environmental diehard tourists, I thought to myself. Soon we found ourselves debating a reasonably serious subject—what should Malaysians do if they want to get greener—buy an electric vehicle? use biofuel? have solar roof? change to new energy-saving light bulbs? I readily agreed with her that all those things could help. But at the risk of sounding ostentatious, I asserted my political opinion on a total stranger whom I just met. 'Actually, the greenest thing we Malaysians can do is this: choose the right leaders! It is so much more important to change our leaders than changing light bulbs.' As if I had gone off on a tangent, Lesley looked at me uncertain whether she should take me seriously.

Noticing the puzzled look, I continued to state my point. 'Why, you might ask? Because leaders write the rules, set the standards, and offer the tax incentives that drive market behaviour across the whole country. Whatever steps we take individually to become greener matter only a tiny bit. But when leaders change the rules, you get scale change across the whole marketplace.' Without waiting for her response, I continued. 'For instance, two or three months in every year for the past twenty years, Kuala Lumpur has been shrouded with choking haze resulting from burning of oil palm plantations, both locally and in neighbouring Indonesia. We have been breathing very unhealthy air, and, consequently, the incidence of asthma and other related diseases climbed.'

'And this has been going on for decades?' Lesley questioned in utter disbelief. 'Seems to me like a simple problem with ready solutions.' With a touch of sarcasm, she further noted, 'And to know that you Malaysians have even sent an astronaut into space.'

'Yes, since 1983, solving this perennial problem has eluded us. When it comes to health and safety and environmental issues, government should be setting standards,' I emphasised. 'What you need are leaders who are willing to push for standards. It is in the long-term interest of the country and its people. So, if you somehow are inspired to be an environment warrior or a green adult after graduating, don't fool yourself. You can change light bulbs. You can use electric vehicles. But if you don't change leaders, your actions are nothing more than an expression of personal virtues. Don't expect to see much change in saving the environment or stopping climate change anytime during our lifetime. So vote smart is the most effective way to turn green.' I profoundly ended our little rap session as I turned my head to steal a look at the line of guests wanting to have their second helpings of delectable grills. I opted to end dinner with a refreshing scoop of ice cream instead.

At night here at Taman Negara, a good thing to do is to stare at the sky full of stars. Without any big city around, the sky is very clear, and you can see many more stars than in any city. The forests around you are pitch black. Not to be seen but only to be heard. Screeching and whining insects. Mating calls of frogs. Sweet songs of nightjars. Before going back to my room, I got bolder and ventured into the forest on my own. Torchlighting the path as I ventured out into the darkness, I came to a halt noticing a pair of shiny eyes on what looked like a dead twig complete with sharp thorns alongside—a unique creature disguised as a twig. It was a stick insect. Amazingness. I also spotted a butterfly resting on a leaf blade, absolutely no fluttering this time. Perhaps deep asleep? I walked up and touched its fragile wings only to see it fleeing into the darkness. I scanned the riverbanks just above the waterline. A luminescent pair of eyes caught my attention. Could have been any reptile or amphibian—presumably a frogs, snake, or lizard out hunting after dark along the edges of the river. Criss-crossing the beam of torchlight, I could picked out bats snatching insects in flight or diving to the water's surface for a quick drink. Indeed, Taman Negara's nocturnal sights and sounds at the waterfront were an opportunity not to be missed. You not only see the rainforest but hear it too. I had a great night's sleep after walking off the calories from the barbeque dinner.

Spending a few days exploring Taman Negara, you come to realise how often it rains in the rainforest. As the thick black cloud rapidly thickened above, little forest birds, the ioras and the flowerpeckers, flirted and darted, taking notice of the threatening downpour. Taman Negara today serves its role in the conservation and understanding of Malaysia's biodiversity. It has been set aside to preserve the country's rich natural heritage and to provide secure breeding grounds where its fauna and flora can thrive, safe from the conflicting interests of a growing human population. 'We have always taken the path of pragmatism in the stewardship of our biodiversity,' explains Dr Zaaba, the deputy director of the Wildlife Department. 'We are committed to low-impact, sustainable flow of visitors to protect Taman Negara from irreversible damage whilst at the same time creating a first-class ecotourism destination.' The Wildlife Department and tour operators here seem staid in ensuring that both tangible and non-tangible rewards of conservation are delivered and shared by the indigenous people and villagers living in the proximity. 'We are working hard to ensure that local communities here have a sense of ownership and vested interest in the future of Taman Negara,' smilingly assured Mr C. C. Yong of Tahan Tours. Reputed for innovative tour packages that feature both adventure and nature education, Yong has been a familiar face here at Kuala Tahan for many years now. 'We often go the extra miles in encouraging the people here to participate meaningfully in promoting ecotourism. We educate them on the services and responsibilities expected of them so that they can reap sustainable financial returns from park visitors. Many locals are employed within the parks by lodges and tour operators.' Taman Negara is today internationally recognised as the primary bastion of global biodiversity. In this respect, Malaysia has a central responsibility to the rest of the world. It is the country's most extraordinary investment into the future. So far, it has effectively served as a lifeline for animals that would otherwise face extinction by human hands. With everyone's support, these vital ecosystems will be preserved for the benefit of our future generations. This way, our oldest rainforest is safeguarded in perpetuity for its intrinsic worth and for the beneficial use and enjoyment of the public. Its preservation is a matter not just of national interest but also of our future survival.

In numerous scientific expeditions, many of my colleagues from the Department of Wildlife and National Parks (PERHILITAN) and Universiti Kebangsaan Malaysia (UKM) had explored in depth the richness of this precious rainforest conservation showcase. Home to a long list of endangered indigenous species, Taman Negara had emerged as a premier destination to those who would like to catch a glimpse of Malaysia's big mammals such as the Malayan tigers, Sumatran rhinos, Asian elephants, and wild cattle gaurs or seladang. More than 200 mammals have been documented in this reserve alone, including sambar deer, barking deer, mouse deer, wild boars, Malayan tapirs, clouded leopards, leopard cats, sun bears, civets, bats, squirrels, tree shrews, and an interesting range of rare nocturnal primates like slow loris, flying lemurs, and tarsiers. Over 300 species of birds were found here, along with more than 300 species of reptiles and amphibians. The reserve was also a haven for seriously inclined botanists with more than 14,000 plant species documented here. Arguably, Malaysia's Taman Negara is one of the world's oldest rainforests. It has continued undisturbed and remained unspoiled for at least 130 million years; meaning, it is older than either the infamous Amazon or the Congo rainforests. This vast expanse of pristine lowland rainforests today represents the most important protected area in the Peninsular Malaysia.

LOVE SONGS WITH A BOOM

UPON MY RETIREMENT FROM UNIVERSITY Malaysia Sarawak (UNIMAS) in 2004, I moved back to Peninsular Malaysia to hold a new position at Malaysian University of Science and Technology (MUST). Whilst that was exciting, I was clueless as to how I could continue my passion of exploring the rainforests and coral reefs like what I have been doing for more than four decades in Sabah and Sarawak. Almost definitely my outdoor activities would never be the same again. Dare I say, the pristine rainforests, magnificent mountains, and amazing coral reefs in these two states have been my raison d'être for having spent almost four decades of my academic career there. I was quite apprehensive about accepting the new job in Kuala Lumpur initially. But I figured there must be enough natural areas in Peninsular for me to get close to nature albeit not quite the same as on Borneo Island, the third-largest island in the world known for its wealth of species and tropical ecosystems.

As I had expected, my wanting to get out of the frenetic hustle and bustle of city life could not have come soon enough. I was feeling the work pressure of starting a new research university only weeks into the new job. It was close to a meltdown. After a few months into my new job, I began to doubt if I had made the right decision. I was dead sure spending more time in green spaces might be just what the doctor would have ordered. The health benefits of being close to nature with all its natural sounds could help me stay both objectively and subjectively facing the new challenges. Objectively, I needed to consider my goals and what I was actually aiming to achieve in this job. I must be cautious about weighing the benefits. I could also choose to be subjective about it. My decision would be very much influenced by my personal feelings, preferences, and views. Either way, concrete debates, the pros and cons, needed to happen in my head. I needed to satisfy myself if I have been right to have accepted this job. I needed a break to reassess my situation. I was only in my late fifties then. So I wasn't entirely seeking for a job that would be easy on my well-being or my health. Slowing my heart rate and reducing my blood pressure weren't featured as primary considerations when I opted for this job. But I was wrong. Within a mere half a year on the job, I was so stressed out. This new job of starting a research university wasn't a walk in the park after all. MUST was to become a research university in collaboration with Massachusetts Institute of Technology (MIT), one of the foremost universities in the world. Dealing with haughty personalities from such a reputable institution wasn't easy, I soon found out. It didn't take long for me to find their arrogance and snobbery most condescending. It was beginning to wear me down fast. Those high-and-might professors and officials from MIT would never understand the research needs and priorities of Malaysia as a developing nation. MUST was not MIT. The path to making MUST a prominent research university would never be as easy as cut and paste on a computer. A drop in the levels of stress hormone cortisol in my system would definitely help to lessen the perceived frustration dealing with the egocentrism around me. I needed to get into a good mood if I were to continue with my job.

Kuala Lumpur and its suburbs had always been a verdant visage to me. Noises emanating from the roads and side streets were loud and ear-splitting. Business for eating places and shopping malls seemed to be on twenty-four hours a day, seven days a week, all the time overpatronised, overcrowded, and overly distracting. Traffic congestions spewed out lead and fumes into the already humid and still city air. Smoulders of invisible noxious gases were causing niggling irritations to my eyes and throat. Even the botanical beauties of bright-orange *Ixoras* and deep-purple *Bougainvilleas* along the main toll roads appeared smothered and struggling to thrive. The air pollution problems I had to contend with seemed infinitely serious and ultimately debilitating, I was sure! 'This friendly city, once the quintessence of unblemished urban living, was no longer,' I resignedly concluded. I felt the need to be away from the levels of anthropogenic sounds of city vehicles, factories, loud music, and people in general. Even public city parks were not spared from the emissions of millions of vehicles plying the dizzying network of toll roads and highways. I was constantly coughing to clear my throat. My mind was already jaded and bored with towering skyscrapers and dazzling neon lights. They have failed to pique my enthusiasm in just a short time after moving here from the lush green environs of Borneo. I desperately yearned for a peaceful ambience. I needed to be close to nature again.

One fine weekend, I decided to tag along Professor Kamaruddin and two of his graduate students on a field trip to Fraser's Hill. I first knew Kamaruddin as a fresh graduate who joined Universiti Kebangsaan Malaysia Sabah Campus when I was the dean of science in 1983. I took interest in this ambitious young man who had chosen lecturing as his goal. He had completed his undergraduate studies in botany then. At his job interview, he impressed me as a highly committed and intelligent person. Like me, he grew up in a small village in Kelantan, having parents who didn't speak any English. Only Malay was spoken at home. Unlike me, who went to school where English was the medium of instruction, Kamaruddin was taught in Malay both in school and university. I figured it would be an uphill task for him to shine as an academic if his command of English remained poor. With the help of a Fulbright professor John Beaman, who was in Sabah then, I managed to get him accepted to do his doctoral studies at Michigan State University despite scoring just the required bare minimum in TOEFL. After four years in the United States, Kamaruddin came back with a PhD in Botany and also a recognisable American English twang of the Midwest, USA. Amazing what someone who had never learned to swim could do when thrown into the deep end of the pool!

'Everyone set for a productive field trip?' asked Kamaruddin excitedly as he finished mucking around finessing the air-conditioning controls of his four-wheel-drive vehicle. After some fiddling, 'Dancing in the Dark' by Bruce Springsteen came out blaring from his car stereo. I muttered a sarcastic assessment of his choice of music, clearly a taste he had acquired after being educated in the States. Having settled comfortably on the front passenger seat, we were ready for a meandering road trip up Fraser's Hill. The morning was slightly overcast, but it should allow a pleasant ride up. The heavy unseasonal downpour the day before had damaged some stretches of the roads. But the robust vehicle did not encounter any major difficulty negotiating the many potholes and wet corners along the winding roads. Kamaruddin wasn't a bad driver after all. In fact, the slower speed he was driving at gave us a better chance to peer out of our moving vehicle and spot a few interesting highland bird species resting on bare branches and power poles leading up the road. We had teasing glimpses of Fraser's Hill avifauna including the unmistakable red-bearded bee-eater (*Nyctyornis amictus*). A pair was seen flying and stopped to perch on a tree. Their coarse chattering call was quite easily distinguished. Sign of their breeding activity was evident from our ability to spot a few couples noisily pursuing and ruffling each other along the paths of the foothills.

A pair of instantly recognizable red-bearded bee-eaters perched on branches patiently waiting to hitch flying insects.

One and a half hour of road travel and a few more sharp corners took us right into the town centre of Fraser's Hill. Nestled at 1,524 metres above sea level, Fraser's Hill has an all-year round temperatures of between

17° and 25 °C. Situated in the state of Pahang, it is approximately 104 kilometres from the capital city, Kuala Lumpur. With a small population of about 1,000, life here revolves around the charming town square resembling that of a Scottish village. The picturesque townscape consists of colonial-style buildings that serve as post office, police station, clinic, tourist information centre, several inns, cafes, and restaurants. A small clock tower stands proudly smacked in the centre. Brilliant blooms of English-style country gardens against the green hues of towering pine trees add to the refreshing ambience of this resort town.

Indeed, the cool and crisp aura of Fraser's Hill was a breath of fresh air away from the smogs of KL metropolitan. Since it was planned as a day trip, we jumped right into business. Kamaruddin and his two graduate students seemed very familiar with the cool primeval forest environment here. The surrounding forests had long became popular weekend spots to be close to nature. It has long been one of the most established highland tourist areas in Malaysia.

Our team of four reached a consensus to walk along one of the many established trails and explore. It soon became apparent to me that this team of botanists from Universiti Kebangsaan Malaysia was very familiar with the many existing nature trails found here. They not only seemed to have a good knowledge of where certain plant species could be found but also were reliably on the ball if any eventualities were to crop up. So I was happy just to tag along with the crowd. The primary purpose of the trip was to look for a rare parasitic plant, *Balanophora*, the subject of study for Kamaruddin's two research students in our company that day.

Balanophora is amongst one of the most unusual genera of all higher plants. It possesses no leaves, stems, branches, or roots. Only its inflorescence can be seen protruding above ground. Unlike the other more well-known parasitic tropical plant, the *Rafflesia,* which grows only on specific host plants, *Balanophora* is less specific in its choice of hosts. Our knowledge on the biology of this plant is still scant. It would be a very fruitful excursion if this team of botanists was to find any new locations of

Balanophora today. I, however, adopted a lackadaisical attitude. It would be awesome if we were to find them in the field today because I have never seen this unique plant before. But if by the end of the day we were to go home without spotting any, I would be happy to be with the team relishing the experience of being close to nature again. The sounds of nature were beginning to calm my inner self. The entire cool ambience was definitely lowering my work-related stress of MUST. I was seizing every opportunity to acquiring that mental state. I closed my eyes and just listened, totally embracing the elements of nature. The sounds of water, birdsongs, wailing insects, calling frogs, and wind rustling through the leaves—they were equally soothing to my ears and mind. Subconsciously, the nagging woes and annoyance of my new job vanished from my head. As a scientist, I found myself rationalising the evolutionary advantage of this positive outcome in humans. It was suggested that our ancestors associated the sounds of nature with a safe environment. The presence of sounds of nature was a good indicator of a safe environment.

The genus *Balanophora* is a parasitic plant shaped like a small golf ball covered with thousands of tiny female flowers. It attaches to host roots by means of hard tuber from which the gorgeous bright red inflorescence arise. It is believed to emit a faint sweet odour resembling that of mice.

All of a sudden, I heard something crashing through the trees above my head. Everyone stopped and tilted their gazes up, way up. I spotted an outline of a slender graceful figure with black furs moving amidst the foliage. It was a siamang (*Symphalangus syndactylus*). I was able to recognise its lean, long, super-strong arms. The arms are twice as long as the legs, a morphological characteristic of lesser apes. These exceptionally long arms enable him to swing much like a pendulum, grabbing one branch and releasing it before grabbing the next. Repeatedly and with absolute ease, the body is freely projected through the air. How fast can they go? An estimate puts siamang able to travel up to fifty-six kilometres per hour. Siamang is also known as the great gibbon because it is the largest of all other gibbons. At their largest, they can reach one metre tall and weigh around fifteen kilograms. That would be twice the size of other gibbon species, though still small compared to the world's great apes such as orangutans and chimpanzees.

Siamangs reside in the gibbon family of *Hylobatidae* but are distinct enough from their relatives to claim their own genus, *Symphalangus*. They are found only in the rainforests of Indonesia, Malaysia, and Thailand. Latest survey shows that siamang populations are rapidly decreasing because of extensive deforestation in recent times. The conservation status of this species is now placed as endangered.

Molecular data suggest the gibbons and Siamang are as different from one another as chimpanzees are from humans. Siamangs however showing more vigour and strength capable of adapting to a wide range of habitat conditions. They are also have webbing between the second and third toes and a dilatable hairless air sac in its throat not found in gibbons.

Waking up for the day, visitors to the Fraser's Hill would become immediately aware of the presence of gibbons around through their haunting songs. They are invariably entertained by the dawn chorus of siamangs emanating from the lush green backdrop of highland rainforests. Like other gibbons, siamangs howl and sing to mark their territories.

The entire enclaves of the eastern valleys seemed to echo with their songs. I tried to figure out the ringing 'melody' in my head. Got it! I began to get the characteristic rhythm of their wailing and screaming. The loud shrills would continue for about ten minutes, gradually rising in the pitch, and eventually peak to a long-drawn crescendo at about every fifteen-minute intervals. They would sing for hours with such series of rising and falling notes. This mesmerising chorus could be heard in the form of duets between males and females. Way yonder from the mist-shrouded valleys, a large male would be energetically hooting away sounding like a bugle tune of a military post announcing the arrival of enemy troops in the battlefield. These calls would always be followed by a loud 'boom' sound at the end of the song. I knew then I'll never forget a siamang's call anywhere and whenever I am in a tropical rainforest again.

Siamangs have a greyish or pinkish throat sac they use to produce loud resonating calls. which they inflate during vocalizations. The throat sac inflates during vocalisation becoming as large as a grapefruit.

Each group would protect its own area of the forest. At the same time, they would be fortifying family bonds, protecting the best fruiting trees, and advertising for a mate. Unlike other gibbon species that often start singing at dawn, siamangs tend to begin a little later. The song bouts would usually peak between 9 a.m. and 10 a.m. Understandably, this late routine could be deafening and annoying if you are trying to continue dozing in your morning slumber. But to most visitors here, siamang's vocal tones range in between the haunting Javanese bamboo flute and the blaring screams of a city police siren. A strange arrangement of a musical piece indeed. Notwithstanding, siamang's incredibly graceful acrobatic abilities plus the elaborate repertoires of melodious duets have rightly earned this primate family the moniker 'the singing, swinging apes' of the tropical rainforests.

So far, no *Balanophora* came to sight. Admittedly, I was more of an animal person than plant. As an undergraduate at Otago University, New Zealand, I found botany laboratory classes humdrum and less glamorous. Zoology was more my thing. So I was paying little attention to what was on the ground. I decided to continue observing the lone Siamang feeding away in the canopy above. He appeared unperturbed by my company. Adjusting my binoculars to its highest magnification limit, I tried to observe as clearly as I could this solitary individual that seemed to get closer to our team on the ground.

Two features distinguish the siamang from other gibbons. The features of their hands and feet make siamangs different from their gibbon brethren. Their feet have evolved to fit the purpose. The two digits on each foot, the second and third toes, are partially joined by a membrane. This is the first of the two distinguishing features that separates siamang from other gibbons. Hence, it is assigned a separate species, *syndactylus*, from the ancient Greek *sun,* which means 'united', and *daktulos,* which means 'finger'.

The second feature that differentiates siamang from other gibbons is the presence of a large gular sac, also known as throat pouch. This bizarre-looking globular skin is located just below its chin and found in both males and females of the species. Siamang's ability to produce loud resonating calls is due to the possession of this sac that can be inflated to incredibly disproportionate size during singing. The sac creates a deep 'boom' with the mouth open and a loud 'wow' sound with the mouth closed. The sight of the large gular sac hanging below its chin reminds me of the occurrence of similar structure in other faunal species as well. Quickly recalling some of the images I have seen in nature book, I am aware of similar throat sacs filled with air found in frigate birds, grouses, and frogs. Generally, the sacs in these species act as amplifiers of sounds they make for specific reasons. But none could perform close as efficient as that of the siamangs. When fully inflated with air, its throat sac can expand to be larger than its own head, giving its song a bagpipe-like boost. This would significantly increase both the volume and range of its calls to be heard all across the valleys. This large inflatable throat sac makes the deep booming calls that can be heard up to three kilometres away. Duetting pairs combine these deep sounds with high-pitched barking notes and occasional bitonal screams.

Siamangs don't just differ from other gibbons physically. One of the things that distinguishes them from other gibbons is their distinct parenting style. Studies showed that siamangs are the only gibbon species in which males are heavily involved in infant care. The male siamangs usually start caring for their infants when they turn one year old. Young siamang generally begins sharing a sleeping spot with the male rather than with the mother. This bed sharing with the male is also true when a younger sibling is born. Thereon, juveniles continue to share a sleeping site with the male until they reach four to five years of age. Whilst monogamous pairs and juveniles are the norms in the gibbon social structure, there are studies that show siamang groups can also be polyandrous. This is a situation where several males share a single female. The reason for this might lie in the choice of mating partners that are considered healthy and fit for the continuance of the species. Similar rationale has been proposed for the monkeys that live in harems consisting of several females mating with a big healthy and highly salacious male.

When vocalizing, the siamang can produce two different kinds of notes using its throat sac: a deep boom when it sings into the sac with its mouth closed and a loud "wow" when it sings into the sac with its mouth opened. After repeated calls are made, it would produce a deep boom sound that is carried farther into the forests than the high-pitched wow sound.

Take Five to Be Understood

In any form of communication, it would be helpful to have a stop signal that marks the end the part transmitted. When calling for mates, siamangs sing passionately for some duration from the treetops. Then almost suddenly he would end it with loud boom to signal a break in the song. No one knows for certain the need for this take five. But siamangs are endowed with a large inflatable throat sacs that enable them to make their resonant, low-frequency calls that end with a loud boom sound. Siamang's deep booming calls are one of the loudest natural sounds in the rainforests of Malaysia and Sumatra. The boom sound can travel for three or more kilometres!

In contrast to birders who spent time on these trails looking up in the trees, our team of botanists needed to fix their eyes to the ground. This way, they wouldn't miss spotting the rare *Balanophora* they came to look for. At the same time, they had less of a chance tripping

171

and stumbling over the unsuspected roots criss-crossing our paths. I had walked further along the trail whilst Kamaruddin was giving unscheduled lectures on the variety of plants encountered as the team advanced. His students' attention was full-on even though they might have heard the same old explanations dozens of times before. But that was Kamaruddin in his elements. By nature, he is always passionate about teaching others. It comes straight from his heart, but he can get overly impassioned with the wrong audience or inappropriate timing. At times, I found myself smiling and nodding my head listening to him dishing out his vast knowledge of Malaysian flora anywhere, anyhow, and anytime, solicited or not.

'Here's one' came a less than excited voice of Liza, one of the graduate students studying the distribution of *Balanophora* in Peninsular Malaysia. She was pointing at a peculiar reddish stump under a large dead tree. Instantaneously. I staggered forward and found myself kneeling over a gorgeous globular structure protruding from the ground. Its bright-reddish-orange colour against the dark-green carpet of moss made it look unbelievably stunning. It resembled an ornate miniature pine cones. But the tiny white specks on it made it appear more like a mushroom. I was literally face to face with a gorgeous inflorescence of *Balanophora*. 'How could you maintain such calmness in your voice?' I looked up at Liza, admiring her candid composure after such a fantastic find. In the ensuing few minutes, we spotted at least eight other clusters of similar inflorescence of various sizes around us. I almost trampled on some. They were in various phases of growth. Indeed, I could have passed some of the smaller unopened inflorescence as toadstool fungi instead of plants. 'It's *Balanophora fungosa*,' proclaimed Kamaruddin with a voice that connoted both authority and confidence. Without questioning, his students nodded in wonderment and agreement. Like most other *Balanophoras*, this species lacks the green pigment chlorophyll, and hence incapable of photosynthesising to make its own food. It is a holoparasitic plant. Remaining underground most of the time, it grows on the roots of host trees, relying completely on the host for growth and survival.

Amidst all the excitement, everyone was soon on their hands and knees trying to get the best tight shots of the inflorescence at different stages of development. Just before bursting its display of golden-orange inflorescence, the plant produces less radiant tuberous growths seen on the ground. 'These tubers are food reserves for the plant,' Kamaruddin enlightened all of us. 'They contain a wax-like substance called balanaphorin.' I nodded with raised eyebrows to indicate my appreciation for the extra piece of information. In my head, I silently recalled a factoid I had come across somewhere stating the *Balanophora* wax material is also inflammable and used by the Javanese people in Indonesia as candles and torches.

One of the two students, Liza, was busy taking counts and measurements of the *Balanophora* tubers and blooms. She was seen drawing and scribbling a detailed ground distribution map of this newly discovered colony of *Balanophora* in Fraser's Hill. I stood back and found myself silently admiring how assiduously they were measuring and noting every possible factor that could have contributed to the growth of *Balanophora* at that particular location. It was an absolute pleasure to see students busy at work getting research data for their thesis in the field. Nothing beats being in the natural habitats of your subject of study, something I've been missing ever since I left Sabah and Sarawak. Kamaruddin is also an avid photographer. Whilst his two student were engrossed in scientific pursuit, he was busy getting snapshots of the rare plant. I knew he was an excellent nature photographer having seen images of plants and animals in his Flicker account on the Internet. Cross-referencing between them, the three big fans of *Balanophora* spent a good full hour before feeling satisfied with all the necessary field data they needed to have. I felt the closeness between Kamaruddin and his students. His students referred to him as Pak Din, an endearing and respectful way to call your teacher in accordance with the Malay custom observed in the villages. But the students assured me they would address him as Professor Kamaruddin when on campus in keeping with the formal address widely expected in recognition of his academic status as a quintessential professor of botany.

Meanwhile, the giant gibbon seemed to get increasingly curious about our presence and had been advancing closer to see what we were up to. He peered down at us, still howling. With his massive throat sac ballooning, he didn't appear to be intimidated by our presence at all. But I was sure he was uncomfortable finding us in his territory. We looked up to watch for several minutes as he used his long, lean, and super-strong arms to fling himself through the canopy with athletic ability. Periodically, he stopped to shake the branches and stared down at us. He gave us that steely gaze; I could just read what it meant in his grumpy-looking face. He was saying, 'Yes, I see you guys down there in my territory. Stay away, intruders. I'm not afraid.' We didn't stay long, not wanting to disrupt his feasting on the juicy figs found in abundance up in the treetops that time of the year. From that moment, we didn't get a glimpse of our lone siamang again on our remaining walk on the trail.

Babies of Siamang are almost hairless at birth. Its gestation period is approximately seven and a half months and a single offspring is born every two or three years. Siamangs reach maturity by the age of six or seven and a female rarely gives birth to more than ten offspring in her lifetime.

In the Land Cruiser headed for home, the conversation was a bit subdued. I noticed the two students were slumping in the back seats, leaning against the car doors, clearly exhausted both physically and mentally. Simply too much excitement for one extended morning field work. Sensing that, Kamaruddin didn't even attempt to feed them with more academic details of *Balanophora*. Furthermore, the road down Fraser's Hill at that hour of the day had started to become too busy and required his full concentration driving. He must take responsibility of getting all of us home safely through that one and only meandering road back to the city.

My thoughts switched back to the enthralling moments with our rainforest host siamang that morning. It would have been more absorbing if it continued serenading us with its songs all the way home. But the two girls were deep asleep by now. His swinging performance was enough to mesmerise. I wondered how old he was? Would he be able to exhibit similar stance with absolute grace and agility as he aged in the wilderness? The siamang is known to live to around forty years in captivity, longer than most species of gibbons. But this turned out to be a curse in disguise, not a blessing. Its remarkable long life in captivity made siamang most sought-after as pets. So much so, the illegal pet trade of baby siamangs had taken a toll on its wild populations.

Rafflesia tengku-adlinii is a parasitic plant species discovered on Mount Trus Madi in Sabah, Malaysia in 1987. The Rafflesia is unique in the plant kingdom for not having its own roots, leaves or stem but gets its nutrient by attaching itself to a specific host plant found growing in undisturbed tropical rainforests.

But siamang's principal threat to the survival of the species is habitat loss. The palm oil production industry in both Indonesia and Malaysia has resulted in unprecedented rates of rainforest clearance over the last few decades. It has substantially decimated their natural habitats as a result. Siamangs aren't alone in this respect. Of the sixteen gibbons recognised by the IUCN Red List, one is categorised as vulnerable, eleven endangered, and four critically endangered. Not a single gibbon species can be considered safe, and some are already on the precipice of extinction. Today, the majority of the world's remaining endangered siamangs can be found in Sumatra, the epicentre for deforestation in Southeast Asia. Additional populations are found sparsely distributed in Peninsular Malaysia and Thailand. There are still debates about whether siamang populations in Sumatra and those in Malay Peninsula and Thailand represent separate subspecies. Primatalogists have nominated Sumatran siamang as *S. s. syndactylus* and the Malay Peninsula and Thailand Siamang as *S. s. continentis.* In these wild habitats, the siamangs are found to occur sympatrically with other gibbons; in other words, they can be found entirely within the combined ranges of the agile gibbons and the lar gibbons.

In their rainforest homes, siamangs play a vital role as seed dispersers. They have been shown to defecate seeds whole and undamaged hundreds of metres away from the parent plants. This helps to give new growth of their favourite fruit trees in their own habitats. If siamangs were to be removed from their own habitats, these seed dispersal services would be lost, leading to the degradation of the forests in the long term. The forests in itself would not be able to support thriving populations of siamangs. Despite their ecological importance, siamangs and other gibbons receive little conservation and research attention. When protection of wildlife species is discussed by wildlife conservation experts, they almost invariably revolve around issues affecting just five iconic species: orangutans, proboscis monkeys, pygmy elephants, Malayan tigers, or Sumatran rhinos. The plights of siamangs and other gibbon species sadly all too often go unmentioned. They have been largely ignored by conservationists, scientists, and the global public even as they are facing many of the same perils as those other big mammals. This disregard could have come partly from Western society's long familiarity with the bigger species such as rhinos, tigers, and elephants. These celebrity species have long become synonymous with wildlife conservation in the tropical regions. The familiarity has been in the English-speaking world for many decades largely because of stories originating in Africa or South Asia. Prior to the 1970s, almost nothing was known about the behaviour or ecology of Siamangs and other gibbons. Perhaps one of the biggest reasons why siamangs and gibbons had been overlooked was their unfortunate designation as being the 'lesser apes'. This term was originally given to the gibbons to indicate their small body size relative to their 'great' ape cousins, not at all because of their lesser importance. Regrettably, the 'lesser ape' label might have been misconstrued as their deserving less urgency and importance for protection. The label made siamangs and gibbons seemed less charismatic, less interesting, and simply less appealing than the so-called great apes. A similar fate seemed to have befallen many of the world's medium and small wild cats such as the Central American margay or the African golden cat. These species had long been ignored by conservationists and researchers, even as they, like the lesser apes, drifted from being safe to endangered in their own habitats.

As I am writing this piece on siamang, I'm having a big lump in my throat. I'm sure as hell I'm not growing a throat sac like siamangs. But I'm teary eyed feeling so sad that Kamaruddin is no longer with us. He succumbed to kidney cancer thirteen years ago. I can still recall the day he was lamenting about his aching back during our last excursion together in Lanjak-Entimau Forest Reserve in Sarawak prior to that. On returning home, he was admitted to UKM Medical Centre, where I visited him with a few colleagues. He was calm and collected, full of stories about fascinating plants encountered on our many past expeditions together. True to his reputation as an impassioned dedicated botanist, he was still giving 'lectures' energetically, not quite aware that he was under the influence of heavy doses of morphine to ease his pains. Mere days after our visit, Kamaruddin passed on.

My utmost admiration to the guy. Malaysia lost a great educator, a prolific botanist, an avid photographer, and a computer wizard to boot. Forever etched in my mind was the particular hot afternoon during the month of Ramadan in 1987 when three of us, Datuk Tg Adlin, Kamaruddin, and I, ended on Crocker Range, Sabah, to accidentally discover the thirteenth species of rafflesia. We named the new species *Rafflesia tengku-adlinii* after Tengku D. Z. Adlin, who piloted us there in a helicopter. Rest in peace, Kamaruddin.

Rafflesia tengku-adlinii is a parasitic plant species discovered on Mount Trus Madi in Sabah, Malaysia in 1987. The *Rafflesia* is unique in the plant kingdom for not having its own roots, leaves or stem but gets its nutrient by attaching itself to a specific host plant found growing in undisturbed tropical rainforests.

HOT ON THE TAIL OF MAN

THE LARGEST PLAYER IN MALAYSIA'S timber industry is a statutory body, the Sabah Foundation, which holds a 100-year timber concession of 973,000 hectares (9730 square kilometres), more than ten times the size of Singapore. The foundation was established in the 1960s with the primary purpose of providing education and training of Sabah human capital to bring economic progress to the state. It was deemed important for Sabah to be at par with other states that it has joined to form Malaysia in 1963. Forested areas were harvested with gusto thereon for their timbers to bring revenues for the development of the state. By late 1970s, much of the allocated timber concession areas have lost their pristine status because of man's short-sightedness, ignorance, and greed. Amongst these areas was Danum Valley, located smack within the timber concessions allocated to the foundation. By mid-1980s, Danum Valley stood as one of the most seriously threatened ecosystems in Malaysia. Its pristine rainforests became highly vulnerable to clearance and harvesting of its high-valued hardwoods for export. Accessibility to this timber-rich valley had been made more and more possible for other exploitations including wildlife hunting. Poaching of the critically endangered Sumatran rhino, *Dicerorhinus sumatrensis,* was reported on the increase. The rhinoceros horn was able to fetch insanely high price for its purported medicinal value. In the meantime, the forest covers on all sides of Danum Valley continued to significantly decline as a result of extensive road constructions for logging activities. Politicians kept calling for more timber harvests to get rapid and maximum more bottom line gains. Those in the corridors of power mounted more and more forest clearance. Huge funds needed to develop Sabah in the name of economic progress, so they told the ordinary people. The cliché 'use it or lose it' was wantonly used to justify their greed. The people on the streets started to pressure the government to stop logging excessively for the sake of the environment. Clear rivers had turned coffee-coloured in the interiors. Settlers along the rivers were not happy with their source of water, which became increasingly polluted and silted.

Then winds of change suddenly came. Something happened out of the blue. The Sabah Foundation moved to put aside a substantial portion of its timber concession as conservation areas. Danum Valley was announced to become strictly a rainforest reserve for the purpose of research, training, and conservation. It was classified as class I conservation area, which meant the area was to remain unlogged, undisturbed, unexploited in perpetuity. A field research station was to be constructed there complete with accommodation, research, and training facilities. They needed to have excellent facilities that could attract researchers from all across the globe. A ground-breaking decision indeed.

I was included in a team appointed by the Sabah Foundation to conceptualise the field research station in Danum Valley. We chose one of the most established and prolific rainforest research stations, La Selva Research Station in Costa Rica to emulate. A team headed by the late doctor Clive Marsh was sent by the foundation to study the facilities and operation there for a couple of weeks. We came back with a clear idea to model Danum Valley Field Centre (DVFC) after La Selva Research Station. In 1986, Danum Valley was ready to welcome scientists to conduct rainforest research from all across the world.

Today, DVCA is in safe hands. With its protected area status, this magnificent ecosystem is effectively sheltered from all human activities and possible adverse impacts. Human encroachment into the forest reserves for agriculture or settlements are kept at bay. Shifting cultivation, wildlife hunting, and logging within its boundaries have all come to a grinding halt since its designation as a protected area for almost four decades now. Much knowledge has been uncovered over the years—about how our rainforest ecosystem works, our plants and animals, where they are, and what are threatening their existence. More than 800 scientific publications have been generated from research in these conservation areas. In 2016, in Zurich, at a major international conference on tropical ecology, Danum Valley was voted second most influential field research centre in the world. Barro Colorado Island, established in Panama since 1950s, was first. Danum Valley, established in 1985, came second, beating its own model, the world-famous La Selva, Costa Rica field centre, which came third.

During the construction of the research station, I used to frequent the forest areas targeted for the building of accommodation and research facilities. This was to ensure the contractors were not wantonly clearing forest areas more than necessary. Indeed, this rugged terrain covering 438 square kilometres of pristine rainforest was a showcase of rainforest biodiversity. The myriad of both animal and plants species here was astounding. Bordered by two rivers, Sungai Danum and Sungai Segama, DVCA's immense size made it the largest lowland protected area in Malaysia at the time. To attract foreign scientists interested in doing rainforest research, I used to go around bragging about it being equivalent to the size of Singapore. It also boasted one of the world's most complex ecosystems harbouring millions of tropical species. The 60-million-year-old rainforest was home to many endemic floral and faunal species found only in Borneo. The majestic lowland dipterocarp forests extended over 90 per cent of the DVCA with trees towering to amazing heights of forty to seventy metres. In terms of species diversity, over 200 tree species were known to occur in a single hectare plot of DVCA, ten times more found in similar-sized temperate forests, which would be around ten to twenty tree species.

On one particular occasion, I was walking along on a forest trail newly made passable by the contractor of the project. The heavy downpour just turned to drizzles. There was no man-made disturbances whatsoever. Even if there had been some inevitable cutting of trees in the process of making the forest trail, the cleared areas were amenable to normal regeneration processes. I found myself thinking how the forests around me had remained lush and green for millions of years. Peter Ashton, a prominent American researcher of rainforest ecology, once explained the process to me. Under normal circumstances, fierce storms could have blown over and uprooted huge trees down. This had resulted in huge forest gaps and widespread over the years. But these naturally occurring gaps allowed light to penetrate all the way to the ground, drastically changing the air moisture of the forest floor. Ideal conditions for seed germination and tree regeneration were then created. Local microclimates in these areas encouraged growth of plants seeds that had remained dormant for years. In time, natural forest gaps would be filled up again. As I was thinking about this gap-filling processes, I noticed something sitting quietly on a branch about thirty metres ahead. I reached for my binoculars and was absolutely thrilled to see a male orangutan that appeared to be sheltering from the recent downpour as well. It was my first sighting of an orangutan in the wild. A moment forever etched in my memory.

Orangutans, *Pongo pygmaeus*, are found only in the forests of Borneo and northern Sumatra. In Malay, its name orangutan means 'man of the forest'—the largest ape in Asia that is astonishingly humanlike both in appearance and expression. Orangutans on these two islands differ in their fur colour and also facial features. The ones in Borneo consistently have darker furs than those in Sumatra. Evidence are accumulating to suggest they could be of two distinct subspecies. They are found in diverse habitats including mangroves, coastal swamps, lowlands, and mountain forests. In Sabah, Borneo, they have been seen at elevations as high as 2,000 metres on Mount Kinabalu.

Adult male orangutans develop large cheek pad known as flange. Why some males develop flange and not others is still unclear. Flanged males appear to show dominance and mate with many females. They also feature strongly in male-male competition competition for access to sexually receptive females.

Unlike the other great apes, the chimpanzee and gorilla, orangutans are by nature solitary. They are sociable like the monkeys and langurs but would also quietly go about the treetops looking for food on their own. When not totally alone, they would travel in small groups, usually a mother with her baby or in the company of a male partner. This solitary nature of orangutans has found its mention in ageless legends told amongst the native tribes of Borneo. One relates how an orangutan stole a human bride and dragged her into the forests. She bore him a son who was half human and half ape. One day, the woman who had been held captive escaped with the child in her arm. She fled to a riverbank where hunters had moored her a boat to escape. But the ape was at her heels. The woman dropped the baby to delay her captor. Whilst the ape paused to pick up the baby, the woman escaped. The ape threw such a rage that he tore the child in two—threw the human half into the receding boat and the ape half into the jungle. Ever since, the orangutans had been roaming singly in the forests.

Orangutans live predominantly on trees. Despite their large size, weighing as heavy as eighty kilograms, they can travel effortlessly through the middle and lower storeys of the treetops. They use their long and powerful hands and feet to full effect. To grasp branches within reach, orangutans use their extraordinarily huge toes in a similar fashion we use our thumbs. In a similar way, their toes make them more mobile and adept at grasping tools. They are able to hang on to branches with just one foot, leaving their hands free to seize any fruits in sight and handy.

Adorable and constantly contemplative look of a young orangutan baby reflects curiosity and eagerness to learn. They stick around with their mother until they reach around 7 years old. During that period, they learn everything they need to know about surviving in the wild from her especially what to eat and how to be weary of predators

The orangutan's diet consists of about 60 per cent fruits. They face tough competitions for fruits in season with other more agile primates like gibbons, siamangs, langurs, and macaques. Other fruit-eating mammals like squirrels and birds would also be going after similar sources of food up above within the canopy. In this respect, an orangutan has two distinct advantages. It is equipped to deal better with hard-shelled or prickly fruits than other fruit eaters. Whilst others often struggle or fail to prise the fruits open, orangutans would do that with relative ease. Their massive teeth and jaws are well suited for opening hard-shelled and spiny fruits.

Visitors to the tropics often fail to fathom how durians, the football-sized prickly fruit with the strongest 'off-putting' smell, can earn the title 'the king of fruits'. The disagreement about durian smell ranges from that of sweet almond to rotten onion. Not everyone can agree to the taste of its creamy flesh either. Despite its deeply offensive smell to most Westerners, durian is top favourite on orangutan's menu. Hence, this hairy ape becomes indispensable in the dispersal of durian seeds in the rainforests. In fact, most wildlife enjoy durians as a delicacy too. Unlike other rainforest fruits, durian does not produce visual signals in the form of brightly coloured fruits to get noticed by potential seed dispersers. Instead, durian advertises its presence by smell. The fruits would fall to the ground when fully ripe. The rainforest inhabitants seem unanimous on the exquisite delicious taste of its flesh. Besides orangutans, other animals of the rainforest like the squirrels, hornbills, mouse deer, sun bears, and even tigers love durians. A mad scramble would follow amongst potential seed dispersers wanting to have a feast of this much sought-after king of fruits. In this competition, the orangutans seem to have the edge. Evolution has given this ape huge jaws wide and powerful enough to prise open the durians. The robustness of such jaws and teeth also means orangutans don't have to wait for the fruits to be fully ripe and soft to get to the edible parts. In general, this ability to feed on unripe fruits would be their winning factor in the competition for food with other species.

Cruelty and abuse at the hands of humans continue to befall orangutans. Adult and babies of this adorable species are sold to breeding centres in Egypt and Thailand, public zoos and private individuals. Instead of being loved and cared for, traded orangutans sold to those acting only for themselves are often mistreated as their owners coerce and train them to perform before crowds or behave like a pet.

Orangutan babies seem constantly playful and gentle. But they grow up to display remarkable cognitive skills able to commit to memory the shortest routes leading to specific trees that bear most fruits at different seasons of the year.

When fruits are scarce, orangutans have been observed to supplement their diet with young leaves, tree barks, and woody lianas. They also devour ants and termites. Occasionally, they might even resort to stealing eggs and babies of birds or squirrels from the nests. Bizarrely, they have also been seen coming down to the ground to eat mineral-rich earth dug up by elephants or other wild animals to supplement their diet with trace elements.

Most intriguing about orangutan's feeding behaviour is their uncanny ability to locate fruiting trees, especially their favourite fruits of all, the durians. They seem to acquire the knowledge of seasons and have sharp memories about the exact positions of flowering trees in that vast rainforests. This way, they are able to predict when different trees will be fruiting for a particular season. They also watch the movements of flocks of fruit-eating birds such as pigeons and hornbills to lead them to fruiting trees. The subject of knowing how primates get from A to B has attracted interests of scientists. Information here might lead to understanding the evolution of cognitive functions in humans. How do we first acquire the mental ability to know where and when to travel in the most efficient way? This might be revealed through knowing how orangutans make travel decision-making, like which way would be the fastest way to get to the durians in season? To do all that would require all the five cognitive processes known in us humans: thinking, knowing, remembering, judging, and problem-solving. For all we know, orangutans might actually possess all these higher-level functions of the brain that could lead to language, imagination, perception, and planning just like humans.

Most wildlife species invest much energy and time to care for their young ones. They nurture their young until they are weaned, providing them with the technical know-how about surviving in the wild. Food gathering and staying safe from predators seem to be their preoccupation in instilling basic skills for survival. In the tropics, the monkeys and apes do not experience perilous weather conditions. Hence, lessons in staying safe under harsh weather conditions aren't as important as with temperate or polar species of animals. But orangutans have been seen sheltering from torrential downpours of tropical rains and lightnings under makeshift umbrellas of banana leaves.

A long learning curve is required for a baby orangutan to acquire enough living skills to be independent in the wild. It seems an evolutionary advantage that an orangutan female reaches sexual maturity around 8 years and bears a single baby every three years, which is the longest birth interval of any land mammal.

In Borneo, there exist no lurking tigers in the wild. Here, orangutan's chief enemies, especially the young ones, would be the clouded leopards and large pythons. To escape from predators, orangutans sleep in the trees at night. At dusk, almost every day, an orangutan would seek a suitable forked branch, making sure it presents a good look out over the surrounding forests before starting to build a nest. It would pull live branches and gather barks to build a nice, comfortable springy nest. A roof might have to be added on to shelter itself from the heavy tropical downpour. Amazingly, this nest building behaviour is not learned or acquired from observing their parents. But orangutan's nest-building seems to be an innate behaviour or inborn. An orangutan that escaped from London Zoo built itself a perfect sleeping nest in a tree in Regent's Park, despite having had no experience to witness nest building with live branches in all its years living in captivity at the zoo.

Itinerant Existence

Each night, homeless people in cities use cardboards laid down on hard grounds or concrete pavements to make comfortable beds. Living on the streets can be a humiliating and dehumanising experience for these people. Like the sleep-anywhere habit of the homeless, orangutans, too, build makeshift beds every night. They use barks, branches, and leaves instead of cardboards. But the primary objective is the same—to get a comfortable night's sleep. Far from being a necessity of abject destitution, the orangutans do this as a lifetime habit.

Once a good fruit tree has been located, an orangutan would spend the entire day within the canopy savouring the find. A mother-child pair would be sharing a large fruiting tree, barely moving more than a few hundred metres in a day. At the end of the day, each orangutan would build a nest of branches and twigs folded down onto a firm branch. They rarely use a nest for more than one night, preferring to make a fresh bed every evening. The nest, however, could be used to rest up or take a nap during the day after a feed in the forests. They would also choose to build away from fruit tress where they have been feeding. This way, they reduce their chance encounter with potential predators that usually sneak up on animals on trees they have been feeding.

In the mid-1980s, I used to tag along biologists counting nests of crocodiles and orangutans. We did the survey using a four-seater fixed-wing aircraft. It is a fast and fun way used to estimate their populations in the natural habitats. We would fly low and try to spot the nests from above. For crocodiles, we would be straining our eyes looking for mounds scattered amongst the dirty brownish water of the wetland or peat swamps. For orangutans, we would be spotting darker green spots of gathered leaves within the lighter green backdrop of the canopy. It was quite straightforward for the crocodiles. The number of nests counted would be a good estimate of the lowest range of crocodiles nesting in the area surveyed. But it was less obvious for the orangutans. The number of nests counted may represent lesser number of individuals in the population. This was because we could be counting more than one nest built by one individual over a few nights.

Like humans, orangutans produce few but well-cared-for offspring. This is clearly a superior reproduction strategy in contrast to many animal species that produce many offspring but with high mortality. A female orangutan reaches sexual maturity at about eight years. She then would be able to bear a single infant about every three years for the next twenty years. A successful female would raise not more than four or five young ones in her lifetime. When a female orangutan shows readiness to mate, she would take notice of the long-distance call of a male and seek out for him. The pair would remain together for several days or even months. During this time, the males behave aggressively towards other males who might try to violate his boundaries. But as soon as the female becomes pregnant, she would resume her solitary life. She would be roaming about either alone or in the company of her older brood. After each delivery of the baby, she would continue to live without sexual interest for several years before attempting for the next one.

Female orangutans make proverbially good mothers. They care for their young longer and more devotedly than any other mammals, barring humans perhaps. During the first year of life, the infant is constantly in physical constant with the mother. The mother-child relationship is especially intimate. The proverbial 'monkey love' is well epitomised here. 'Mouth-to-mouth' contact becomes more than ever tender expression of the affection between mother and child. The baby would be completely weaned only after three years of age. Only at three to seven years old, the half-grown animal gradually separates from the mother and starts to spend longer times alone. They would no longer share their mother's nest after a new baby is born.

Orangutans produce few but well-cared offspring. Infants are so attached to their mums that they ride on her body and sleep in her nest until they develop their own skills to survive on their own.

The male essentially has nothing to do with raising the infants. He would move on to a new territory and try to impregnate other females. But recently this widely held notion of male orangutan playing no role in caring of their young appears misleading. It is true that in the wild, motherhood might be priceless and unconditional, whilst fatherhood is conspicuously absent. But in captivity, male orangutans seem to break this rule. He is far from being heartless and uncaring. In Denver Zoo, Colorado, United States, a two-year-old infant orangutan unexpectedly became motherless. A male orangutan, not the biological father, stepped up to play the role of a mother, bearing full responsibility in raising the orphan. This was never seen before. Undoubtedly, this unusual case took those studying primate behaviour by surprise.

A pleading look of a male orangutan shows concern for their future. A century ago there were more than 230,000 orangutans in total, but now an estimate between 55,000 and 65,000 wild orangutans left. Habitat loss alone has pugnaciously made orangutan reproduction plummeted to a level beyond recovery of their fallen numbers. They are now classed as critically endangered species.

Today, it is believed that there are still more than 15,000 orangutans living in the wild. They are still sensitive to the destruction of their habitats and become more vulnerable to being hunted. The only safe orangutans are the roughly 20,000 individuals living in the national parks and protected areas in both Borneo and Sumatra. Estimates put the figures at 85 per cent found in Sumatra and the rest in Borneo. They are now protected by law in both Indonesia and Malaysia for more than fifty years. Nevertheless, young orangutans are still traded illegally in large numbers. To get a baby orangutan, the mother will have to be killed first. Many of the baby orangutans died in transit. For each infant that ends up in Europe and the United States alive, there would be at least five or six dead orangutans. The traffic must be stopped.

Some urgent measures are needed to responsibly deal with the orangutans confiscated from people who have kept this endangered species as pets. Some happen to be baby orangutans left orphaned after their mothers were killed in fires set ablaze during forest clearance by humans. In the 1950s, the authorities in Sabah and Sarawak started to confiscate orangutans from their captors, dealers, and owners. In 1965, a rehabilitation centre was established in Sepilok, Sabah, a protected forested area where orangutans were cared for. On arrival at the station, the confiscated animals would be placed under quarantine for at least one month. During that time, blood and faeces of the animals were checked for the presence of any disease agents. This was to ensure they were free from any diseases of human origin that they might in turn infect wild orangutans upon their release. Here, they were exposed to learning and imitating other half-wild orangutans that would come to feed at the centre. They would learn the skills of climbing and swinging on the lianas around the station. At the centre, a few feeding platforms were constructed around huge tree trunks, where previously released semi-wild orangutans would come to feed. Only milk and bananas were given day in and day out. The diet was deliberately kept monotonous for a reason. This way, the animals would be driven by their own motivation to discover other food varieties from the nearby forests. They would learn from others what other types of food can be harvested from the forests and where to look for them. It would be a time for discovery by trial and error. With the passage of time, they would become more assured and more venturesome. At least this was the intended outcome the centre would like to see. Some ardent animal conservationists were sceptical and apprehensive with this method. Concerns were raised about released orangutans from the centre—that they would not really get rehabilitated to successfully survive on their own in the wild. In 1967, these worries were suddenly proven unfounded. The first sign of rehabilitation success was evident when a female orangutan, after an absence for some time after her release to the wild by the centre, brought her firstborn to the centre. That showed released individuals, despite being 'spoilt rotten' under human care previously, would be able to survive on their own in the wild. They were still capable of finding food independently, evade potential predators, and even reproduce.

These youngsters, the new generation of world citizens, are reminding us that this planet Earth belongs to them too. We are lethally choking the one and only planet we commonly share with them. Tropical forests are the principle and most effective buffer against climate change. Setting fire to the tropical rainforest has a double impact on global warming that ultimately would drive all inhabitants of this planet to extinction.

This Sepilok Orangutan Rehabilitation Centre has long been practically synonymous with orangutan viewing. For decades, this coastal town Sandakan on the eastern side of Sabah has been drawing wildlife enthusiasts from across the globe for a face-to-face encounter with the most recognisable conservation icon, the orangutans of Borneo. This has been seen as a boom in Sabah ecotourism as more tourists come here to gain deeper understanding of humanlike apes and watch their humanlike antics in the natural environment. The surrounding forests at the centre also offer an opportunity to discover the wealth of flora and fauna found in this part of the world. The primary rainforest here has been protected and conserved by the Sabah Forestry Department since the English colonial days. One could explore through a network of jungle tracks available for walking at leisurely pace suitable for visitors of all ages. Besides the universal fans of orangutans, the pristine primary forests also welcomed nature lovers for bird-watching and photography. Some might come here to simply seek solitude and peace.

Once I accompanied an old friend from Michigan, USA, an avid thinker and fervent researcher, here to marvel at this remarkable ape. Amidst the 'oohs, oows, and how cute!' shrieks of excitement from the entertained crowd, my dear friend was busy declaring, 'It would be man's greatest loss if orangutans continue to be under threat and driven to extinction!' He put his rationalisation in the most serious fashion typical of an academic. 'Studying orangutans is extremely important!' he proclaimed and continued to enlighten me in the most profound fashion, making that day one of those moments I have not forgotten till today. Amongst his list of salient points are as follows. Orangutans remain the least studied of the four great apes. They are humankind's closest relatives, sharing some 97 per cent of our DNA. If these noble great apes were driven to extinction, as now seemed likely, that would mean more than the tragic passing of another adorable animal on Earth; it would also mean losing some potential understanding of ourselves. The study of orangutans is starting to achieve startling new insights into some of our most fundamental questions: What made us men and not monkeys? When precisely did that divergence occur? And, even more intriguing, what lit the spark of learning and sharing of knowledge that eventually became mankind's bonfire of culture and science? In the wild, groups of orangutans share distinct 'tricks of the trade' for feeding, nesting, and communicating. They are innovative tool users, a skill that is taught by one generation to the next, not inherited. They also demonstrate a much higher degree of cooperation in daily tasks such as finding food and sharing them. They have social skills like grooming and family bonding. These behaviours represent humanlike culture. To researchers like my Michigan friend, these are momentous discoveries giving new insights into the beginnings of culture. Indeed, culture is the single greatest distinguishing mark of humanity. Culture provides us with a huge evolutionary advantage over our less friendly cousins of the rainforests. It is the same sort of sociability and cooperation seen in orangutans today that early humans had been able to harness as the mechanism separating us from the beasts.

Give us back our forests! In less than two recent decades, close to seven million hectares of pristine rainforests disappeared in Borneo, a decline of close to 15 percent.

I was left dumbfounded and totally impressed with my friend. He was dead serious, and right too. I have had an earful from a fellow academic who seemed very passionate about orangutan conservation but for the cause I have never really given much thought the way he did. I have not reached such intense and learned level of rhyme and reason why orangutan must be protected from becoming extinct. From that moment, I have not stopped thinking a great deal about orangutan and culture.

We used to hold the notion that we alone in the animal kingdom manufacture and use tools. This is now known to be untrue. Jane Goodall famously struck the first blow to this falsehood when she showed evidence of chimpanzees making tools to fish in the wild. Since then, the floodgates have opened. Wide-ranging examples of tool using in the animal kingdom have been video-recorded and documented in scientific journals. Literally, sticks and stones do not break their bones. Asian elephants have been observed to systematically modify branches to swat at flies off their huge bodies. Otters employ stones to hammer shellfish off the rocks and crack the hard shells open. Crows improvise hard slender sticks to spear grubs in tree holes and carefully pull them out for food.

To no surprise of behavioural scientists, primates stand out amongst mammals as the most frequent tool users. Gorillas have been seen employing upright poles to test the depth of river water before wading to cross. Macaques living in temples are known to pull out hairs from visitors' heads and ingeniously use the hair as their dental floss. In the wild, groups of orangutans share distinct 'tricks of the trade' for feeding, nesting, and communicating. Scientists say these behaviours represent humanlike culture. The discovery offers tantalising new clues about our own evolution. Studies had revealed that some orangutans are avid tool users. They employ short sticks to shave stinging hairs from the fat-loaded fruit of the neesia tree. This is a momentous discovery. To primatologists, they have really discovered the beginnings of culture. This is a skill that seems taught by one generation to the next, not inherited. In other words, the orangutans do have culture. This blurs the line about culture being the single greatest distinguishing mark of humanity. Orangutans also have a much higher degree of cooperation in daily tasks such as food sharing and grooming. This higher sociability allows orangutans to teach one another how to access the fat-rich fruits more efficiently. This alone provides them with a huge evolutionary advantage over their less friendly cousins that don't share or cooperate with each other. It is this same sort of sociability and cooperation amongst early humans that have been the mechanism separating us from beasts. On tool using, orangutans seem to be just a step ahead than other primates. Like other apes, they have been observed to use tools in procuring food.

There have been video evidence of orangutans using a sharp stick to accurately spear fish whilst precariously hanging from liana vines over rivers. They have been filmed measuring the depth of water with a stick and use it to steal fish caught in a net.

Interestingly, orangutans may be the first primate known to use a tool for communication. They have learned to create a new kind of distress signal using leaves to lower the pitch of their common warning calls. The resulting sound is known as a kiss-squeak. By putting leaves between their lips, orangutans apparently make themselves sound bigger and more threatening. The improvised whistles emanating from a bundle of leaves in their hand essentially serve as a tool to ward off predators. Young orangutans take to emulating this kiss-squeak signals quite early in life. Hence, this tool using is a means of communication passed along to the next generation. When knowledge and skills for survival are passed on such as this, it is defined as a culture. This is an epic and most compelling evidence that culture isn't something unique to us humans after all.

A quick glance into an orangutan's almost human, emotion-charged eyes, there's no denying that these red hairy apes are our intimate kinship. Orangutans are naturally the most intelligent of the great apes. They're so close to us, we can learn a huge amount about our own physiology, psychology, and early origins. Just like us, their level of sociability goes much higher than the use of tools: they share food and help one another in tasks such as food collection. These new findings are just beginning to reveal what we will lose if wild orangutans become extinct. Often dubbed the world's best field botanists, orangutans are also talented pharmacists, treating their illnesses with forest plants. Because of their similarity to humans, the benefits are obvious. Seeing such resourcefulness and existence of culture brings us to question our old notion that intelligence is exclusively ours as humans.

The worrisome face of a species at the brink of extinction. Orangutan are endangered by human actions. Is there reason to be optimistic for their future? Perhaps we can heave a sigh of relief to learn the rate of rainforest loss is on a declining trend today and numerous effective conservation measures have been put in place. But this optimism should not make us rest on our laurels. More knowledge on the status and threats to the primate species are needed for us to ensure the perpetual existence on planet Earth.

There has been excitement all round amongst researchers studying behavioural science. A powerful window has now opened up to help us learn what capacities and other cognitive functions we might possibly share with these arboreal cousins of ours. The sight of an animal making and using a tool captivates us, especially when culture seems evident in the primate world. The most wonderful moments in my encounters with monkeys and apes are seeing their cheekiness. Ability to outwit humans would be a serious breakthrough in our attempt to gain more understanding of human behaviour. Humans can predict our own action by figuring out what we see and hear. We are clever enough to read the minds of others. Then we would use this skill to their own advantage by intentionally deceiving or manipulating whether others can see and hear them. It has long been speculated that primates are sufficiently clever and can be sneaky this way. They are suspected to be more aware of other's perceptions than we realise. I have seen instances when they behaved badly, they would crouch down, sneak away to the side, and then snatch the food. This indicates that they can read our mind and intentionally plan their deception. They have knowledge of what others can and cannot see and hear. So they do have far greater awareness of what others know than we have previously anticipated.

Human beings are often said to be different from other animals because we have the ability to know ourselves. Animals appear to have a sort of group consciousness, but no individual self-consciousness. This self-awareness enables us to form a concept of ourselves and our own thoughts, allowing us to take into account the minds and experiences of others. Do animals have this sense of self-awareness? The classic mirror test has been used to find this out. When a chimp was given a full-length mirror, it spent the first few days touching the mirror and looking behind it, believing that it was gazing at another chimp rather than at its own reflection. Soon, their behaviour changed. It began using the mirror to view parts of its own body that it would normally be unable to see, such as its own face and the inside of its mouth. This, however, did not mean that it now realised it was looking at its own reflection and thus exhibiting self-recognition. To test it further, the chimp was anaesthetised, and whilst it was asleep, red dye was applied to one eyebrow ridge. When it awoke, the chip saw itself in the mirror and spontaneously touched the marks whilst looking at its reflections. This indicates it has indeed recognised itself in the mirror. Except for humans and chimps, the only species to show self-recognition were the pygmy chimpanzee (*Pan paniscus*) and the orangutan (*Pongo pygmaeus*).

The adorableness of this great ape was also in its unsuspected cheekiness. At the Sepilok Rehabilitation Centre, they have been known to swiftly turn into snatch thieves. They would grab cameras by the straps or mobile phones in people's pockets to just as quickly climb up trees, leaving visitors stunned. Rangers had to eventually remove a tree trunk nearby where these loots were stashed for keep in the hollow by these cheeky monsters. I could still recall an incident when one of my students screamed in fear after one of these onerous orangutans decided to pull her hijab, the head covering the Muslims wore, and ran away with it. But nothing beats an incident vividly related to me by a park ranger at Sepilok. It happened in Sepilok forest when a Caucasian visitor decided to go a little astray from the rest of his tour group busy watching orangutans at the observation platform. He came face to face with an adult orangutan that seemed approachable enough to be photographed up close. But suddenly his mack came under the strong grip of the ape's long hairy arms. Momentarily he was ecstatic at this show of friendliness by his super model. But when the animal started pulling hard at his shirt, he became terrified. When he felt the embrace of the big hairy arm tightening around his neck, he started to panic. The ape clearly wanted his shirt. As the pull got more aggressive, he decided to drop his camera and gave in. He loosened up his shirt buttons and became topless, leaving his shirt on the ground. But the firm, unloosening squeeze of the hairy arms around his naked neck and back terrified him further. The ape wanted more. It started pulling at his shorts now. The poor man was petrified beyond words. Like the wind, he promptly kicked off his trousers to the ground and ran. What a sight! Upon seeing a virtually nude body running wildly in the forest, some local Malaysian ladies panicked as well. They, too, started running, shouting, 'Orang putih gila, orang putih gila,' which literally translates to 'crazy white man, crazy white man,' and started a scramble down the track to the park entrance. This incident was read on TV3 News by then very popular newscaster Wan Zaleha Radzi. It got the whole nation amused, shaking their heads at how cheeky our arboreal cousins can be sometimes.

Today, only about 50,000 Bornean and 7,000 Sumatran orangutans remain in their natural habitat. This is perplexing because, as a species, orangutans are able to live a long life like humans. They are known to have survived as long as sixty years in captivity. Orangutans share 96 per cent of its DNA with humans. By inference, they should be smart enough to maintain the survival of their own species compared to any other animals of the rainforest. But why are there so few orangutans left in the wild today? There have been many theories to explain this apparent paradox.

Hunting of orangutans dates back as far as 1776 when the first batch of orangutans reached Amsterdam as part of the animal collections of Prince William V. The hunting and collecting of orangutans continued into the nineteenth century by famous naturalists such as Alfred Russel Wallace and Hornaday. In those days, these natural science collectors and distinguished biologists were collecting orangutans with no less zeal that collecting butterflies. They were captured in large numbers—highly valued as trophies and household animals. For at least 35,000 years, orangutans have been hunted for food. It is likely that overhunting by early humans is responsible for the eradication of orangutans in Java.

The low population of orangutans, despite its high intelligence and longevity, is also linked with the headhunting tradition in past Borneo. Once upon a time, taking the heads of other people signified important events that took place in the lives of the Dayak people of Borneo. For instance, a Dayak husband must present a human skull to his wife after the birth of a child. It was a tribal belief that failing to do so would bring harm or endanger their baby with the possibility of illness or even death. Further, a young Dayak man was only deemed ready for marriage not until he had ambushed and beheaded a fellow Dayak or an enemy from another tribe. The victim's skull would then be presented to his potential bride for a hand in marriage. Such were the beliefs in times of yore in ancient Borneo.

When headhunting was outlawed by the colonial dynasty Rajah Brookes before World War II, the population of orangutans in Sabah was said to have significantly decreased further. This timing was of no coincidence. Researchers believed that banning of headhunting imposed by the Rajah after the World War II could have increased hunting of orangutans. The Dayaks were indirectly pressured to headhunt orangutan heads instead of human heads. Young men seeking wives resorted to orangutan skulls instead of human's as wedding trophies. Orangutans were heavily hunted, causing their population in the wild to rapidly decline. Duel with an orangutan was also considered a trial of courage amongst the headhunting tribes of Borneo. A Dayak warrior was required to measure himself against a huge orangutan in one-to-one combat. On the ground, the warrior would mockingly stretch out his arm towards the orangutan. Almost invariably, the orangutan would try to grab and bite off the offered limb. In a flash, the warrior would then cut open the stretched arm of the orangutan with his curved knife and claim victory by killing off his mighty opponent in whichever way he fancied.

Banning of headhunting by the tribes of Borneo could have also emboldened wildlife hunters from outside to venture deeper into the rainforests. Previously they were fearful of losing their heads to the roving headhunters. They stayed away from a large portion of the Bornean rainforest. With the ban on this age-old tradition, the previously untouched forest areas became safer to pass through, allowing killing of wildlife, including orangutans, on a wider scale.

As a result, the population of orangutans that used to exceed half a million at the beginning of the nineteenth century plummeted to less than 50,000 in both Sumatra and Borneo in just half a century. As this cute humanoid species keep losing their natural habitats, human-ape conflicts increase. Primary rainforests were burnt to make way for thousands of hectares of oil palm plantations. In the process, orangutan populations were almost decimated. Indeed, there is no 'silver bullet' solution to the plight of orangutans in rapidly developing countries where oil palm industry remains as the mainstay of their economy. The benefits and welfare of a huge portion of the population of these nations must also come into the equation. The advancement of development and economy is always a function of time. One day, developing countries will progress to emerge as developed nations. It is a matter of time. But for the orangutans, hot on the tail of man, their time is running out.

MUCH TO GAIN, THE ROT MUST STOP NOW!

MAN IS WISE AND CONSTANTLY in quest of more wisdom. It is my belief that the ultimate wisdom remains locked amidst the simple beauty of nature. When we think about nature, our popular notion is it is where we encounter beauty—simply an arena in which beauty is displayed. But nature can also be a very important source of wisdom. What is wisdom? Wisdom is the ability to recognise good and bad; it is not knowledge. There is a crucial difference between wisdom and knowledge. Knowledge is the recognition of cause and effect, which is independent of good or bad. Hence, seeking knowledge involves investigation and discovery, which lie within the realm of science. But it usually takes only a keen pair of eyes to learn and derive wisdom from nature. I never fail to appreciate the cliché 'Knowledge is knowing that a tomato is a fruit; wisdom is not putting it in a fruit salad.'

From time immemorial, mankind have been discovering nature, which has a lot to teach us. From the ancient world to the modern, human lives have been influenced by animals in matters that reach far beyond the food chain. In a Tanzanian jungle, a scientist and a medicine man follow a chimpanzee in search of a cure for a deadly disease. On the plains of Kenya, a woman learns a powerful lesson about family care from a pair of elephants. And in the Florida Keys of USA, an eight-year-old boy with a genetic illness utters his first words for a chance to swim with dolphins. Nature has never ceased to reveal some of the surprising ways in which animals help teach, heal, and strengthen people in body, mind, and spirit.

If nature is full of wisdom, this begs the question, what wisdom can we learn from it? As a scientist, I have learned to appreciate the interrelationships that are found in nature. I have often been reminded, 'In nature, there is no existence; there is only coexistence.' I've thought a great deal about this sentence since I first heard it, and the more I think about it, the more it rings true.

During one of my walks in the rainforests of Borneo, I was introduced to a unique ant-plant mutual relationship that clearly epitomises the coexistence of nature. There are many different species of plants that have a variety of strategies to attract pollinating ants. But this tropical vine *Dischidia* must be one of the most creative. It grows with regular flat leaves for photosynthesis, and it also produces specialised thickened leaves that are hollow on the inside, shaped something like a flask with a small opening at the top. Inside these modified leaves lives a whole colony of ants. Confined inside this tough hollow structure, the *Dischidia* plants provide the ants a safe haven from their enemies. As the ants live inside these leaves, they defecate, and a good deal of ant 'poops' builds up, which is rich in valuable nutrients for plants. *Dischidia* plant has a special ability to grow roots above the ground, sprouting and spreading into these hollow modified leaves to access the growth nutrients in the ant poops.

My second intriguing example of nature's coexistence is also exemplified between ants and plants. There are many species of plants that are home to many species of ants. But a group of plants that does this in a big way is a genus found in the forest called *Macaranga*. The relationship is highly specific with each species of *Macaranga* tree being occupied and patrolled by a particular species of ants. The ants walk along the branches and leaves of the tree and attack any would-be herbivore that seeks to make a meal of the soft tissues of the plant. These ants would even ferociously attack humans who inadvertently lean up against a *Macaranga* trunk or come in contact with its branch. But this is hardly a one-sided affair. In return, the *Macaranga* plants provide small fat-rich globules that the ants ingest, or make small disk-shaped nectaries from which the ants drink. Some plants even have specialised structures in which the ants live. More recent works have revealed that some of these ants will actually leave their host species and venture onto adjacent trees that may be shading their host tree from the sun needed for photosynthesis. The ants would go about actually working hard to cut off the interfering branches to give their tree more direct access to sunlight.

When we look up at the sky and see geese flying along in V formation, we ask why they choose this particular pattern. There is much wisdom to be drawn from here! As each bird flaps its wings, it creates an uplift for the bird immediately following behind. By flying in V formation, the whole flock adds at least 70 per cent greater flying range than if each bird was to be flying on its own. When a goose falls out of formation, it suddenly feels the drag and resistance of trying to go it alone and quickly gets back into formation to take advantage of the lifting power of the bird in front. When the head goose gets exhausted, it rotates back in the wing, and another goose flies in to take the lead. The rest of the flock honk from behind to encourage and motivate one another to fly forward. If a goose becomes ill or wounded by gunshots and falls out of formation, two other geese fall out with the wounded goose and remain with it to lend help and protection. They stay with the hapless goose until it either recovers or dies. Only then do they launch out and return to their group.

So what kind of wisdom can we gain from the above-mentioned ant-plant relationships and V-shaped flying formation of the geese? These are pretty amazing examples of interactions. The first take-home point is that we are also coexisting creatures. We are at our best when we live together, coping with other human beings within an interconnected network of nurturing relationships. Nature has subtly released their innate wisdom into the hearts and minds of mankind, changing our lives for the better. We, too, can get much further if we operate in community, supporting and uplifting each other. Like the geese, at some point in our lives, we, too, need an encouraging honk! It is a universal rule that what we give out will come back. Be willing to really care. If someone needs our help, we'll be there.

Our tropical rainforest is very rich and diverse in species in Malaysia. Its nature is in its primordial form and, therefore, in its prime. It just teems with biological treasures. But the treasure chest is only partly open, as many species are still waiting to be discovered. Knowledge and wisdom remain unlocked. Nature's biodiversity holds an enormous potential in transforming our well-being through agriculture, health, and industrial sectors, lifelines capable of contributing to our economic growth and poverty reduction. The unique species of plants and animals constitute our natural wealth. However, these treasures and diversity are underutilised. They have not been exploited to its full potential.

Biodiversity, with all its richness and diversity of species, comes to us within the realms of tropical rainforests; the oldest ecosystem on Earth of at least 100 million years. During the ice ages, the last of which occurred about 10,000 years ago, the frozen areas of the north and south poles spread over much of the Earth, causing huge numbers of animals to become extinct. But the giant freeze did not reach many tropical rainforests. Therefore, rainforest plants and animals of that era could continue to evolve, contributing to make rainforests as the most diverse and complex ecosystems on Earth. Circling the Earth's equator like a belt, the rainforests offer nearly perfect conditions for life to continue and survive. The tropical rainforests maintain a near constant temperature of 80 °F and receive anywhere from 160 to 400 inches of rain per year. These favourable weather conditions allow all life forms to flourish year-round. A great number of species don't have to worry about freezing during cold winters or finding shade in the hot summers. They rarely have to search for water, as rain falls almost every day in tropical rainforests. By virtue of their location, the tropical rainforests are spared the extreme loss of life that characterises other regions of the globe during the ice ages. These factors help explain why the tropical rainforests are home to between 50 and 70 million different life forms.

More interesting is knowing how millions of animal species manage to live together without running out of food. In the rainforests, it is a continuing pushing-and-shoving match amongst the species in search for food, water, sunlight, and space. It is a wonder how despite such fierce competitions, these many different species of animals can all live together. Ironically, this is actually the reason why a huge variety of different species exists in the rainforest today. Here, many animals have evolved and adapted to eating a specific type of food to survive. By becoming specialised feeders of a certain plant, fruit, or animal that few other species are able to eat, they avoid competition for food. Have you ever wondered, for instance, why hornbills have such big beaks? These beaks give them a great advantage over other birds with smaller beaks. In turn, the fruits and nuts from many trees have evolved with a tough shell to protect them from being eaten. This process of evolution and adaptation went on for millions of years, creating more new species in the rainforests.

Why is biodiversity conservation important? We are constantly bombarded with the need to stop losing our endangered species in the wild. Nowadays, we hear this same old refrain much too often. Some of us may have been desensitised to it. But the world's biodiversity is being lost at an alarming rate that the phrase remains true. In Malaysia, rainforests have been rapidly disappearing because of logging practices and other economic activities. Most of our biodiversity are being destroyed even before we have the chance to scientifically document and study them. Aldo Leopold, the pioneer of environmental conservation, said that each species is a link in the web of life. He emphasised that if some links become extinct, this web loses integrity, weakens, and eventually disintegrates. This implies that every species is dependent on other species for its survival. So it is vital to save all the links even if we are unaware of their connections. The main premise is that humans are part of this web of life. Somewhere along the line, the human race will be affected by such losses. Hence, we need to conserve as many 'links', weak and strong, for our own survival. All habitats and ecosystems of planet Earth need to be conserved so that all the species and their interrelationships remain intact.

Indeed, our biodiversity is a library of genetic information about life on Earth. If the 'books' or species are being burnt even before they are read, we are losing irretrievable information that could have saved us one day—useful natural products that can improve our lives, such as a cure for disease through new or improved medicines. Almost 90 per cent of people in developing countries still rely on traditional medicine for treating their ailments. These medicines are based largely on different species of plants and animals of the rainforest. Tropical rainforest plants are rich in secondary metabolites, particularly alkaloids, which biochemists believe are compounds that protect plants from diseases and insect attacks. Many alkaloids from higher plants have proven to be of medicinal value and benefit to human. They have also contributed immensely in the search for many possible cures of life-threatening diseases in the Western society. Currently, 121 prescription drugs sold worldwide come from plant-derived sources, The U.S. National Cancer Institute has identified 3,000 plants that are active against cancer cells, and 70 per cent of these plants are found in the rainforest. Twenty-five per cent of the active ingredients in today's cancer-fighting drugs come from organisms found only in the rainforest. Despite a quarter of modern pharmaceuticals are derived from rainforest ingredients, less than 1 per cent of its millions of species have been studied by scientists for their active constituents and their possible uses. Plant-derived drugs from the rainforests can be worth a lot. By 1980, sales in the United States of plant-based drugs originating from the rainforests amounted to some $4.5 billion annually. Worldwide sales of these plant-based drugs were estimated at $40 billion in 1990. But these prescription drugs, only 121 in total, sold worldwide come from only ninety species of plants. Imagine the number of possible drugs to be discovered from millions of species that have yet to be studied by scientists for their active constituents and possible uses.

The rainforest treasure chest has hardly revealed its precious content for humanity. Besides medicine, rainforest biodiversity has been our source of food too. So far, it has provided us with at least 80 per cent of the developed world's diet. Its bountiful gifts to the world include fruits like avocados, coconuts, figs, oranges, lemons, grapefruit, bananas, guavas, pineapples, mangos, and tomatoes; vegetables including corn, potatoes, rice, winter squash, and yams; and spices like black pepper, cayenne, chocolate, cinnamon, cloves, ginger, sugar cane, turmeric, coffee, and vanilla, and nuts.

But what have we been doing? Instead of appreciating the many indispensable values to biodiversity, we continue to ignore their invaluable good. We have failed to make the most of biodiversity. The rate of conversion from natural forests to plantations has remained high for many years at our hands. We have significantly reduced the areas of pristine rainforests. In the process, we have created fragmented habitats too small for endangered species like orangutans and gibbons to continue surviving. The reduction of forest land is changing climates worldwide, causing global warming and untold adversities to man and his surroundings. Unprecedented weather patterns and rising sea levels are causing havoc to nature as a whole. All endangered species on planet Earth could have already arrived at historical lows in their existence on planet Earth. Their population is starkly reduced, and many are constantly struggling to survive. Their vulnerability to becoming extinct is in all-time high. Yet humans are adamant at adding salt to the wounds that are clearly festering and worsening.

It definitely looks like we are throwing ourselves under the bus. Rainforests once covered 14 per cent of the Earth's land surface; now they cover a mere 6 per cent. One and a half acres of rainforest are lost every second with tragic consequences for both developing and industrial countries. Nearly half of the world's species of plants, animals, and microorganisms will be destroyed or severely threatened over the next quarter century because of rainforest deforestation. Experts estimate we are losing 137 plant, animal, and insect species every day because of rainforest clearance. That equates to 50,000 species a year. We are constantly reminded the remaining rainforests could last less than forty years.

We are already sensing the global catastrophe in the horizon. Holding sway are our needs for food security, medicines, fresh air and water, shelter, and clean and healthy environment in which we live. We must be more serious in thwarting the rapid loss of our biodiversity and protecting our natural environment. We need to live in harmony with nature. How? This entails setting a target of protecting at least 30 per cent of terrestrial, marine, and freshwater ecosystems around the world. For biodiversity hotspots, including Malaysia, we need to safeguard at least 60 per cent of these areas. This calls for almost a third of the planet to be designated as protected by 2030. To achieve, foremost would be stopping deforestation.

We really need to get across to the laypeople on the streets about the concept of biodiversity itself. What do we mean by biodiversity? How many species do our rainforests support? What are the challenges in our attempt to understand biodiversity? Surprisingly, scientists have a better understanding of how many stars there are in the galaxy than they have of how many species there are on planet Earth. Estimates vary from 2 million to 100 million species, with a best estimate of somewhere near 10 million. Of these species, only 1.4 million have actually been named. Today, rainforests occupy only 2 per cent of the entire Earth's surface and 6 per cent of the world's land surface. Remarkably, these remaining lush rainforests support over half of our planet's wild plants and trees and one-half of the world's wildlife. Hundreds and thousands of these rainforest species are being extinguished before they have even been identified, much less catalogued and studied.

We need to open up new opportunities to exploit biodiversity to our own benefits. In recent decades, biotechnology has increased our food production, stemmed environmental degradation, fought diseases, and added values to our products based on natural resources. Biotechnology can be used as a tool for acquiring scientific knowledge or to intervene directly to increase the productivity of many developing nations to promote industrialisation. In conservation, biotechnology helps eliminate the pressure on loss of biodiversity. It reduces the acts of direct harvesting of plant and animal species from the rainforests. Biotechnology enables the laboratory synthesis of novel compounds and commercial production of new cultivars. Cultivation of these plant and animal species could help save the rainforest from being cleared and destroyed.

Should we leave rainforests pristine and never to be disturbed or exploited? Yes would be the answer if we were to move to the other extreme end of the argument. Rainforests act as the world's thermostat by regulating temperatures and weather patterns. Globally, forests absorb about 30 per cent of greenhouse gases emitted by human activities. Over 11 billion tonnes of CO_2 a year is absorbed by forests alone. With the rapid disappearance of forests, less of the greenhouse gases are removed from the atmosphere, causing global warming and severe weather patterns across the world. Catastrophic consequences have been increasingly evident in recent years in the form of forest fires and rising sea levels. The warming of the Earth is the subject of intense concern of many scientists, policymakers, and citizens of the world. Participants in the debate are often ignorant of the facts and the scientific principles underlying global warming. Understandably, global warming is an incredibly complex subject, and many important facts are not widely known. Besides acting as a critical sponge capable of soaking up CO_2 that heats up the Earth, rainforests are also the planet's richest repository of our biodiversity.

They are critical in maintaining the Earth's limited supply of drinking and fresh water. Nearly 90 per cent of the 1.2 billion people living in extreme poverty worldwide depend on forests for their livelihoods. Fifty-seven per cent of the world's forests, including most tropical rainforests, are located in the developing countries. The higher temperatures in the tropics cause higher rates of metabolism, ecological dynamics, and co-evolutionary processes, which generate and maintain higher biodiversity. To limit global temperature rise, we must start slashing emissions of greenhouse gases. Every country needs to invest now to protect, manage, and restore ecosystems and land for the future. This century's biggest global challenges are twofold: climate change and biodiversity loss. They are intricately interrelated.

By 2100, planet Earth is predicated to hit 3 °C of warming above the temperature prior to that of the industrial era. The 2015 Paris climate agreement aims to limit the global temperature rise this century to below 2 °C. Mitigation measures include reducing greenhouse gas emissions from agriculture, industry, and use of fossil oil for transportation and energy. But many scientists seem to suggest it would be impossible to achieve the target solely through cuts of greenhouse gases. They are less than optimistic that emissions driven by agriculture and heavy industry could ever reach zero anytime soon. For this reason, they are advocating nature-based solutions as an added measure to achieve net-zero emissions and stop further global temperature increases. These innovative solutions partake powerful tools capable of reducing global temperatures in the long term. Climate experts claim nature-based solutions will be able to cool our currently warming planet by the second half of this century. They have long-term carbon-sink potential. The goals would still remain the same—that is, to ameliorate the impacts of rising temperatures on biodiversity, equity, and sustainable development. For example, when biomass vegetation is burnt for energy, emitted carbon dioxide could be retained and stored underground. This process is known as bioenergy with carbon capture and storage, or BECCS. These technologies involve the capability to capture and store CO_2 from the air. It is a technology that came to the forefront of global warming initiatives only very recently. It is hailed as a breakthrough with respect to its appropriateness because it would be very unaffordable to developing countries rich in available biomass. Let us wait anxiously for the successful application of BECCS technology. Its ameliorative impacts on the two biggest challenges for today's world—biodiversity loss and climate change—would be welcomed by all species on planet Earth, not just humanity.

Nonetheless, these resource-rich but technology-poor countries may still practice other cheaper options to reduce atmospheric greenhouse gases. Three ways are currently popular. One is to avoid emissions by protecting ecosystems and, thus, reducing carbon release. Limiting deforestations is most effective here. The second way is to restore ecosystems, such as wetlands or logged-over forests so that regenerated forests can go back to sequestering carbon. The third is to improve land management. These include coming up with prudent policies to ensure our forests are not depleted by the timber industry, our massive fertile topsoils are not impoverished by agriculture and plantations, and our pastures are not overgrazed by livestock. We need to do both: reduce the emissions of greenhouse gases, CO_2, methane, and nitrous oxide; as well as sequester carbon.

We need to be better committed about progressing and improving our well-being on planet Earth. Humans must change their ways. Our economy must be decarbonised at unprecedented rates to achieve net-zero targets by mid-century. We need to be more innovative in transforming social and economic systems that can lead to sustainability. We also need to be resilient in the face of ongoing climate impacts. The whole world, rich and poor countries, must invest now in nature-based solutions that are ecologically sound, socially equitable, and designed to pay dividends over a century or more. Properly managed, these could benefit many generations to come.

Indeed, we are at a crossroad on whether we will fare better or worse in the near future. The many environmental stresses now are going to impact adversely on our social and economic landscape. We have 'missed the bus' to leverage on our rich natural resources in the most beneficial and sustainable manner. Are things going to get a lot worse over the next century? We have been lackadaisical and careless. We have lost the opportunity to quell the previous wave of scourge caused by unscrupulous leaders of our society. We can continue to rant and rave at the government, politicians, and corporations. There sure is enough blame to go around for everyone, but in reality, this is a failure of our own apathy. We have ignored the intricate importance our own ecosystems and environment that have served us well for generations. Greed in the name of economic development has come to the forefront with devastating consequences unfolding in front of us by the very minute.

Globally, forests absorb about 30 per cent of greenhouse gases emitted by human activities. Over 11 billion tonnes of CO_2 a year are absorbed by forests alone. With the rapid disappearance of forests, less CO_2 are removed from the atmosphere, causing global warming and severe weather patterns across the world. Catastrophic consequences have been increasingly evident in recent years in the form of forest fires and rising sea levels. The warming of the Earth is the subject of intense concern of many scientists, policymakers, and citizens of the world. Our policymakers, industry leaders, and politicians are often ignorant of the facts and scientific principles underlying global warming. Understandably, global warming is an incredibly complex subject, and many important facts are not widely known. Besides acting as a critical sponge capable of soaking up CO_2 that heats up the Earth, rainforests are also the planet's richest repository of our biodiversity.

I spent decades as an academic, and over the years, I have known leaders adamant that these adverse impacts are nothing but inevitable collateral damages. Preposterously, they often claim such negative bearings are part and parcel of our pursuit in building a progressive and economically sound nation. This had to happen, they say. However, the answer is much more complex than they think. It is rooted deeply in the behavioural changes required as much as it is about stopping deforestation and altering our ecosystems. There are a number of interconnected concepts underpinning current societal behaviour that we need to be aware of and understand. We need to start thinking of enacting these changes from within. Only then would we be able to see the light at the end of the tunnel. It goes beyond the rhetorical announcements of conservation initiatives and hypocrisy of putting national sustainability policies. Attitude is really one of the most urgent things that we need to address. As much as we exhort these leaders to get their act together, we, too, have an important role to play. There is no room for complacency in education by getting the message across about environmental degradation, biodiversity loss, and looming climate change. We need to instil accurate environmental mindset to become prevalent in a large segment of our society. Truth be told, taking things easy out of over-optimism is not an option. It is going to be a long and tough journey requiring much goodwill and efforts of everyone. A tough nut to crack would be to get the politicians and corporations towing the line. These parties would only adhere to the conservation and environment regulations as long as they are policed. The moment they think they can get away with it, they will keep flouting any and every environment mitigation until caught.

Academics and environmentalists in Malaysia have been in a state of environmental fatigue for so long. They have become exasperated and hugely frustrated seeing exploitation of natural resources done in pursuit of short-term bottom line. The people in power keep violating the sanctity and resilience of nature. Biodiversity is in rapid decline. They fail to appreciate the fact that genes carried in millions of these species were created and tested over billions of years. What we have today has been the result of nature's response to evolution. Evolution is innovation. New and improved genes are created through mutations and preserved through reproduction. Evolution is like a new technology out of which millions of robust and successful species are created. Genes carried in these species continue to be inherited by generations that come after. Their importance is tested over billions of years, ensuring the species continue to survive on this planet Earth. This is the basis for nature's long-term resilience brought about by evolution. Destroying nature is depriving ourselves of the information that we may benefit in ensuring the survival of our own species into the future. Most Malaysian academics of my generation are worn out and totally sapped by the different policies and strategic plans put in place for the conservation of our ecosystem and associated species but never lifted off the ground. This is a worrying predicament. These weary academics are those who had previously been aware, vigilant, and observant of environmental issues but have become fed up. In Malaysia, this has been constantly fuelled by the poor enforcement of environmental policies by the relevant agencies. Planning and execution seem not connected. At the rate we are going, it is a long shot to get us out of the woods as quickly as we wish. All the more reason we need to stop the rot now.

Above all else, we need to remind ourselves how we as humans have become rapacious plunderers and destroyers of other living things on planet Earth. What right have we to do so when other species have been much earlier than us? In putting this question to my students, I often used an interesting way of looking at it as a metaphor. A science writer set the whole process of Earth's existence taking place in one-day period. If we were to put it on a twenty-four-hour clock and 24:00 hours (midnight) as equal to the present time, the dinosaurs were roaming this planet at 22:46. That would translate to just one hour, fourteen minutes ago. When did we, *Homo sapiens,* come to exist on planet Earth? Well, believe it or not, we just came on at 23:59:56.9, a mere 3.1 seconds ago, just before midnight. Looking back at what had happened since 00:00 this morning, we will find that life on Earth began at 4:10 with all life forms found only in the sea. All quiet on the surface of the Earth, till single-celled organisms like yeast and amoeba started to become established at about 13:02, just more than an hour after midday. Still nothing seemed to stir on land till late in the evening. Plants started to grow on land at 21:31, and animals started crawling out of the water at 21:46. The first reptiles, dinosaurs, and mammals came on board between 22:00 and 23:00. The early forms of birds in the sky came on at just after 23:00, followed by humanlike apes just before midnight. It only took less than three seconds before the hairy apes swinging from trees to trees evolved to walk upright, shed their facial and body hairs, and became us, humans. Noting that we have been here on planet Earth only slightly more than three seconds ago, what then gives us the right to call ourselves the 'masters of nature' and be free to exploit nature to our heart's content in meeting our needs and wants?

INDEX

9 781664 107021